GROW FAST
GROW
GLOBAL

GROW
GLOBAL
PUBLISHING

GROW FAST
GROW
GLOBAL

6 steps to unstoppable international growth in the digital age

SARAH CARROLL

CONTENTS

FOREWORD

The Travelwrap Company - The Grow Global Journey

I founded The Travelwrap Company 10 years ago. In the beginning, most of our business was selling through trade via retail shops and department stores who were selling on our gorgeous Scottish cashmere wraps. We were knitting in the UK, which meant that our costs were very expensive and the margins tight. I felt I was working very hard but not making any profit. I was right! I knew there had to be a better way as we had an amazing product that I wanted to share with the world, but I also wanted to make my business viable and reap some financial rewards.

I was introduced to Sarah, and I think our meeting overran by about 3 hours (we hardly had time for a coffee!). I remember thinking it was one of the most engaging afternoons of my business career. Even at the time, it felt like the start of something important and a new stage of my journey. Up until then, our online activity amounted to just a few domestic sales, and I wasn't considering the global possibilities or scalable potential of our business at all. Sarah opened my eyes to both.

I left that day with both a plan and a purpose. I worked really hard with my team at Travelwrap to put in place and implement all of Sarah's brilliant prescriptive advice... step by step, territory by territory. In the early days, we slowly started to see results, and then our business really started to scale. In the first year of implementing the changes that Sarah had suggested, our UK online business grew by over 100% and our US online business by over 400%. We are now seeing steady growth of 50-80% worldwide annually in different territories. I love it when customers call to say our brand is being chatted about as one of the best cashmeres available in NYC or Sydney!

I would like to thank Sarah and applaud her enthusiasm and expertise for helping us to tick those boxes of our online global journey. I am constantly recommending Sarah's workshops, webinars and now her book to any of my entrepreneurial friends who are ambitious enough and brave enough to take on the world. It is a life-changing journey!

Niamh Barker
Founder
www.thetravelwrapcompany.com

ABOUT THE AUTHOR

For as long as I can remember, I have always loved learning different languages. I'm not sure if this was fuelled by growing up on the South Coast of England and looking out across the English Channel as a child, wondering what was over the water (which I now know the French call *La Manche*) or by living with my grandparents in Harrow in London as a toddler, surrounded by the foreign language students they hosted, who spoke all sorts of languages.

While growing up, I went on as many school exchanges to France as I could, and spent long idyllic summers travelling around France with my Nan, visiting some of the students she'd looked after years earlier. I was also thrilled to spend a year at a French university in Strasbourg as part of the European ERASMUS programme.

I just love travelling and am so lucky to have family and friends all over the world. I am at my most happy arriving in a new city, and discovering the language, culture, music, food and drink – and chatting to as many people as possible in any way that I can in order to find out how that new country 'ticks'.

Maybe it's this curiosity, but I have always had a fascination with the way we form connections across borders. When I started working in other countries for Accenture and Deloitte and managed teams with people from all over the world, I became even more interested in how different cultures affected how people did business and worked together. This exchange is sometimes puzzling, but always enriching. Now is such an exciting time for an international enthusiast like me, because it has never been easier to gain a global reach and get your business to potential customers on the other side of the world.

About 10 years ago, I set up Grow Global to help businesses just like yours take full advantage of the global opportunity there is to grow by using digital strategies. I focus on increasing international leads and sales through digital channels. I have worked with over 700 companies on a one-to-one basis and hosted webinars, seminars and workshops with thousands of delegates.

I am a real advocate of going global, and the more people I can tell about it the better (I can literally speak for hours on this topic, as I'm very chatty by nature!). I've spoken at webinars and seminars for global banks like Barclays, HSBC and Santander, as well as numerous Chambers of Commerce, trade exhibitions and trade associations that specialise in all areas of business from music to manufacturing. I've recently been a guest speaker at Google London, talking about digital export, and I'm also keen to help trade promotion agencies to help their companies trade more online, as well as across borders. As a result, I have worked with Invest NI (in Northern Ireland), NZTE (New Zealand's trade promotion agency) and ExporTT (in Trinidad and Tobago).

While working with the UK government's trade promotion agency (UK Trade and Investment and now the Department for International Trade), I've seen how almost 5,000 companies have managed to sell around the world successfully. I've seen what works and what doesn't, and where their stumbling blocks and barriers kick in – and that's what I am going to share with you in this book.

One of the reasons I'm so passionate about growing globally is the transformative effect I've seen it have on businesses: failing businesses have suddenly become incredibly profitable, and businesses that were just about surviving have enjoyed their best year ever and increased their revenue tenfold! My approach to global growth really does work. Global growth is not as complicated or overwhelming as a lot of people think, providing you use digital tools to do it.

My vision is to help more and more businesses sell online around the world. This will increase the economic well-being of each of those companies and their teams, which will, in turn, lead to an increased quality of life for millions of people.

Are you ready to go international right now? Are you ready to use digital to do so?

If the answer is yes – then this is the book for you!

Welcome to the Grow Global digital revolution!

I'd love to hear how your journey to international digital growth goes. Please share your success stories on social media and tell me where you've achieved online leads and sales using the hashtag #GrowGlobal.

I hope you enjoy reading my book.

Sarah Carroll
@growglobal
@iamsarahcarroll

INTRODUCTION

 The digital economy is creating new opportunities for trade and development. It is helping smaller businesses and entrepreneurs in developing countries to connect with global markets more easily, and is opening up new ways of generating income.

Information Economy Report 2017, United Nations Conference on Trade and Development (UNCTAD)[1]

We are living in an age of digital disruption. Digital has managed to shake things up in every part of our lives, from our morning routines to how we run and grow our companies. This stealth invasion may have started small, but the rate of change is now just staggering, and it doesn't look set to slow down any time soon.

Happily, with this disruption comes great opportunity.

Some businesses will struggle to adapt or keep pace with technology, and will ultimately pay the price for this. They may get overtaken by competitors, or find their niche no longer even exists. However, smart businesses will not bury their heads in the sand and look nostalgically to simpler times. They will, instead, embrace innovation and come up with a strategy so that they too can capitalise on the massive potential that going digital offers their business. Nearly 25% of the global economy is already digital[2] – **so, are you missing out?**

By acting today, you have the opportunity to work at the intersection of two hugely underexploited areas: international (increasing numbers of people and businesses are buying across borders) and digital (innovative technology platforms and tools are now available to you in your daily business lives as part of the digital revolution). By combining the two, you will give yourself a head start. Not only will you gain a competitive advantage, but you can also transform the future of your business and reach millions more customers all over the world.

Global growth used to be only for the biggest multinationals, but it's just not like that anymore. Barriers to entry are down and the world is open for business of all types, including yours. You no longer need to staff offices all over the globe, pay commission to expensive local agents, or even to travel the world touting your wares at expos and trade fairs. To have an international customer base, you only need to find a way to sell your goods or services online.

The internet has opened the doors of international trade to everyone. Regardless of the size of your business or your experience of running a business, the process is just the same for everyone. Of course, the specific implementation may be different in each case, but the fundamentals of solid, sustainable global growth are universal, and it is my 6-step method to achieve this that I share with you in this book. This innovative, groundbreaking method I have developed is based on the experience I have had working in the UK with one of the world's leading trade promotion agencies, showing companies how to sell more to customers around the world by using digital channels. Some companies that followed my method have achieved 10x (a tenfold) increase in online revenue, or even more. The UK is one of the most advanced digital economies in the world, so you can learn the tips and tricks of what works and then apply them in your own country. If you are reading this, thinking there is no way you can get your product or service to all corners of the globe or you are too small to achieve that kind of growth, then you are wrong. You can, and I'm going to show you exactly what you need to do. If you don't have the time or resources to sort out going digital just now, then a competitor will probably beat you to it. The time for action is now.

Selling online needs to be an integral part of your business plan for the next three years and beyond. This really is something that you have to invest in, or you will risk being left behind and losing out, both in your home country and in other countries around the world. If you get this right, you will have access to literally millions of new customers without even leaving your desk, and achieve growth by bringing your products and services to the world. On top of this, you will sell at a much higher margin and be able to target your ideal customers more easily.

I truly believe that any company can achieve global growth with my system. Whether you sell a good or service, sell to businesses or direct to consumers, are an established company or a brand new start-up, there is absolutely no reason why you can't be selling online or getting online leads from customers overseas.

Once you master the know-how and digital skills I am going to teach you, you will be able to get ahead of your competition in any country with a sound digital strategy, and this will have the added bonus of improving your online sales and leads in your home market too.

My 6 steps will propel your business onto the international stage. If you think it is just about digital marketing, you are not seeing the full picture. I take a different angle and focus on boosting international digital sales.

I am going to show you how to expand your business internationally online, turn your business into a bestseller and transform your initial investment in your online business by over tenfold.

Are you ready to start your journey to unstoppable international digital growth?

This is truly game-changing.

DIGITAL IS KING. WHAT ARE YOU MISSING OUT ON RIGHT NOW?

The internet is becoming the town square for the global village of tomorrow.

Bill Gates, Microsoft[3]

To get one step ahead of the game, you need to have a solid understanding of the digital landscape. This will ensure that you not only survive, but also really thrive in the digital age. You already know that there has been a digital shake up and the world is changing before your eyes, but you may not know the full extent of what exactly is going on or where.

In Part A, I'm going to fill you in on the key digital trends that you cannot afford to ignore as you grow your business globally to clue you up on the subject. I'm then going to introduce five key international digital sales platforms, as well as the best ways to become visible and get selling to online customers around the world. Not only will you learn what they are, you will also gain insight and clarity so that you can make the right decisions to take advantage of this opportunity.

Are you ready to discover the opportunity that is out there for your business to grow fast?

Chapter 1
The Digital World

 The development of affordable digital tools and platforms has provided new opportunities for micro-enterprises to tap into foreign markets in a way that would previously have been unimaginable.

Entrepreneurship At A Glance, OECD[4]

Without doubt, the digital world is changing before our eyes. The internet has been the biggest leap forward for many generations, and digital technology has changed how customers behave and the way that the world does business. Even very traditional businesses have been forced to adapt their models, such as doctors and lawyers starting to offer consultations over Skype or manufacturing companies that are staffed by robots. To really prosper in this digital age, you need to reach out and sell to customers all around the world.

In this chapter, I'm going to blow your mind with some facts and figures that will show you the vast scale of the potential customers you have access to as a business in the digital age. Everything is going up, from the number of people in the world to the number of people and businesses online. Whether you sell directly to consumers or to other businesses, prepare yourself for a growth spurt.

Internet Explosion = Opportunity Explosion

It is no coincidence that I am writing this book now. Well over half of the world's population is now connected to the internet. The growth in internet users is fast. There has been a huge surge since 2004, when internet users reached 1 billion for the first time.

This rose to 2 billion in 2009, 3 billion in 2014 and 4 billion at the very end of 2017[5].

Scratch below the surface and you will see that your opportunity comes from a number of disruptions that companies all around the world are now waking up to:

- The world population is growing fast
- Over half the world is now online
- More purchases are made online
- Customers use their own languages online
- Customers spend more time online on mobile
- Millions of businesses exist in every corner of the world
- The shift online is from West to East
- New technology platforms are springing up.

So, what is the significance of each of these trends for your business?

The world population is growing fast

There are now over 7.5 billion people in the world, and it is interesting where your prospective customers actually are. Well over half of the world's population is in Asia, standing at 4.5 billion people, compared with nearly 750 million in Europe and over 500 million in North America. In fact, five of the top ten countries in the world by population are in Asia (China, India, Indonesia, Pakistan and Bangladesh). The other five are the United States, Brazil, Nigeria, Russia and Mexico, with Germany being the only European country in the top 20 at number 16[6].

However, population isn't everything. The biggest economies in the world are the United States, China, Japan, Germany, the United Kingdom and France, while the wealthiest include Qatar,

Luxembourg, Singapore, Ireland, Norway, Brunei and Macau[7]. Customers in all these countries have enough disposable income to afford your products and services. Furthermore, in some emerging and developing countries the middle class is growing at a very fast rate, and we are seeing that increasing numbers of customers can afford certain products and services for the first time[8]. In Asia, over half a billion people are already categorised as middle class, which is more than the total population of the European Union. Over the next two decades, it is estimated that the middle class will expand by another three billion people, and this will come almost exclusively from emerging economies[9].

Companies accustomed to serving the middle-income brackets of the old Western democracies will need to decide how they can effectively supply the new bourgeois of Africa, Asia and beyond.

Hitting the sweet spot: The growth of the middle class in emerging markets[9], EY

What does this mean for your business?

The location of your customer base is changing, so your customers of today and tomorrow may not be from where they were in the past. As the internet reaches more people and the middle class grows in developing countries, so too does demand for most products and services. Picture your ideal customer: think about which countries they might live in today, and then which countries they might live in in 10 years' time. Today, it might be Singapore, but in 10 years' time it could be Nigeria. With rising purchasing power right across the world, you cannot afford to be static, so keep an open mind from now on about where your customers are.

Over half the world is now online

There are now 4 billion people online, which means that over half the world is using the internet. We reached this turning point in 2017.

Traditionally, the USA is considered to be the internet pioneer, as it started the dot com boom and produces some of the digital giants of today, such as Facebook and Google. But the biggest concentration of internet users is actually in Asia. With nearly 2 billion internet users, it has half of all the internet users in the whole world (only about 17% are in Europe, 10% in Latin America, 10% in Africa and a tiny 9% in North America)[10]. Not only that, Asia has the fastest growth in volume of people coming online, as well as the largest number of people using the mobile internet. Think about that for a moment and ask yourself what you could be missing out on.

Looking more closely by country, China and India have the most internet users, with nearly 750 million and over 450 million respectively. This is perhaps not surprising as they have the two largest populations in the world. What is incredible, however, is that only 50% of the Chinese population is online today, and only about a third of the Indian population, so there are millions more yet to connect to the internet. It's only going to get bigger! The next highest number of internet users is in the United States, where there are about 287 million internet users, which puts things in perspective. Nigeria, Indonesia, Mexico and Bangladesh are now in the list of the world's top 10 countries by internet users, alongside China and India. There are some surprising growth hotspots, so do your homework before you make assumptions about where to sell online.

> *There are now no European countries in the top 10 countries by internet users. The UK was overtaken a long time ago, as were Germany and France. Both the UK and France used to be in the top 10 when I first started researching these figures five years ago, and Germany was too until midway through 2017.*

What does this mean for your business?

The potential is vast. You can reach customers online in markets that you may not have ever considered doing business with before. While these may not be the first countries you would think of trading with, or be the easiest to do business with right now, I want you to be aware that the locations of your potential customers online are shifting considerably, generally from West to East. Make sure that you are in a good position to take advantage of the Asian internet boom. Act now so you can gain first mover advantage.

More purchases are made online

Both consumers and businesses are increasingly making purchases online. While a lot of the limelight has been taken by the selling of retail and consumer goods to consumers online (B2C), it is in fact the mega growth of online sales between businesses that is taking centre stage (B2B). Although slower to start, B2B sales are expected to be ten times larger than online sales to consumers (B2C), as more and more B2B companies turn to selling online[1].

The facts of the matter are that worldwide e-commerce sales in 2015 reached over US$25 trillion, 90% of which were in the form of B2B e-commerce and 10% in the form of B2C sales[1].

In particular, retail sales worldwide rose by 23% in 2017 to over $2 trillion and now account for 10% of total retail sales worldwide. China and the USA between them account for nearly 70% of all global e-commerce[12]. When you're thinking about countries you could sell to online, remember that China is the biggest e-commerce market in the world and a country where selling through e-marketplaces is very popular. Although online selling is more mature in the USA, it is still growing fast year on year and nearly everyone there shops online. Next comes the UK, which surprises a lot of people. The UK is one of the strongest e-commerce economies in the world and UK consumers have the highest spend per person. Next comes Japan, where mobile commerce is widespread. Germany, which is currently seeing some of the fastest online growth in Europe, is in fifth place.

Mobile commerce already dominates in China and India, where it accounts for more than 70% of e-commerce sales, as well as in South Korea, where the figure is 59%. In Germany, the UK and the USA, m-commerce will account for about one third of all retail e-commerce sales[13].

When we look at sales between businesses, it is clear the e-commerce market is nearly ten times bigger than the B2C market at over $20 trillion[1]. Generally, the majority of companies selling B2B are about five years behind their B2C cousins. The move to more B2B e-commerce is being driven by a number of factors. These include automation and operational efficiency, as well as customers demanding a better online experience, as we have all got used to excellent online websites and experiences in our personal lives.

The USA is the most advanced nation in terms of B2B e-commerce sales, followed by Japan and China. The others are South Korea, Germany, the UK and Russia[1].

> *By 2021, it is predicted that retail sales will be about $4.5 trillion, which will be around 15% of all retail sales. It is already higher than this in some countries. For example, in China, 19% of all retail sales are already via the internet, and this figure is 14% in the UK[12].*

What does this mean for your business?

There is an absolutely massive opportunity to grow your business fast, but the majority of that potential is currently in the USA and China. Imagine if you could get your business to grow at a rate of 25% a year, year-on-year, and what difference that would make to your bottom line. If you are selling online to businesses, then you still have a chance to catch up and get ahead of the curve, as I estimate that most B2B e-commerce websites are at least five years behind retail sites. Whatever you sell and whoever you sell to, you will need to make your business agile enough to adapt to change as new markets and opportunities open up.

Customers use their own languages online

Although English is still the most widely used language online, with nearly 1 billion internet users[11], the internet is clearly not just in English. In fact, Chinese-speaking internet users are very close behind with over 750 million users. Every year we see predictions that there will soon be more Mandarin Chinese speakers using the internet than English speakers, but it has not quite materialised yet.

Between them, English and Chinese account for roughly 50% of all internet users worldwide. They are a long way ahead of the other world languages that are widely used on the web, such as Spanish, which is used by over 300 million internet users. After that comes Arabic, Portuguese, French and German. Interestingly, as all of these languages are spoken in more than one country, they are classed as world languages. English, for example, is spoken in over 100 countries, while French is spoken in more than 50 countries around the world (albeit some of them are small beautiful islands in the Caribbean and Indian Ocean) and Spanish is the official language in over 20 countries[14].

It is actually unusual for a country to be monolingual. Many countries have large numbers of second or even third language speakers, as many nations are bilingual or trilingual. For example, there are 11 official languages in South Africa and 22 in India. In the case of English, it is estimated there are well over 1.5 billion speakers with a working knowledge of the language[15], and while French has only 76 million first language speakers, there are over 350 million French speakers worldwide. Take Canada, for example, where about 20% of the population is French speaking[16].

Because of this, it is likely we will see increasing numbers of languages widely used on the web, as internet penetration increases in certain geographic regions. Although Hindi and Bengali are in the top 10 languages spoken in the world, they are still underrepresented online, as two thirds of India has yet to come online. The fastest growing languages on the web are Arabic, Russian, Malay, Portuguese, Spanish and, of course Chinese, all of which grew by over 1,000% between 2000 and 2017[10].

> *The USA is now the second largest Spanish speaking country in the world after Mexico, with nearly 43 million native speakers and 15 million who speak it as a second language[17]. It is expected that the USA will have the largest Spanish speaking population in the world by 2060, with nearly one in three people speaking Spanish there[18].*

What does this mean for your business?

You need to communicate with customers in their own language, as well as take your time to adapt your products, services and messages, so that they are tailored to your local audiences in their languages. To start with, there is huge potential to do business online in just your own language. For example, English reaches up to 1 billion customers and might well be enough for your business! A website in Spanish cannot just target customers in Spain, but can extend to those in Argentina or Chile too. You can reach half of the world's internet population by having your website in English, Chinese and Spanish. When you are ready, select one of the more widely spoken 'world' languages, like French or Arabic, to tie in with where you are planning to do business. It's a big ask to work in lots of different languages, so if you're not ready, don't fudge it or do it half-heartedly. Instead, it is best to stick to selling to customers who speak your own language first.

Customers spend more time online on mobile

Not only are more and more people coming online around the world, but they are also spending more time connected to the web. People in Thailand, the Philippines and Brazil spend more than a staggering nine hours a day online, with half of that time spent on mobile phones. The USA comes in at 6h 30m spent online, with 2h 14m on mobile, while the UK is close behind with 5h 15m online, with 2h 1m on mobile[19]. This phenomenon is skewed by age, as the under-25 age group spends much more time on mobiles, and 70% of the world's youth are already online[20].

We are becoming addicted to our smartphones. In fact, mobile use has now overtaken desktop use, with over half of the world's internet users accessing the web from their mobile phone. In addition, over half of all web page views worldwide are done via mobile, more Google searches take place on mobile devices than on desktop computers[21] and 9 out of 10 people access social media via their mobile[19]. The countries where the greatest number of people use mobile phones are South Korea, Hong Kong, Italy, Singapore and Poland[19]. Generally, only about a third of customers worldwide complete a purchase through mobile, but over two-thirds browse the web with it in order to make their purchasing decision and track delivery[22]. Online purchases through mobile are now nearly $800 billion worldwide. This is one of the fastest areas of digital sales, with nearly 1 billion people using their mobiles to buy from websites, online marketplaces or social media networks[23].

> *Mobile is now the gateway to the internet for billions of citizens across the world and will be responsible for connecting millions of currently 'offline' global citizens to the internet in the years to 2020 and beyond.*
>
> Anne Bouverot, Director General of the GSMA[24]

What does this mean for your business?

Your customers are **already** online by using any device they can find. It's that old adage about going to where your customers are rather than getting them to come to you. It is not just Western millennials who are hooked on the internet, it is changing how people spend their time and make buying decisions the world over. You just need to get in front of them on the screens they are glued to and connect with them, whether that be on Amazon, YouTube, Facebook, eBay or Google, or heads down staring at their email. It sounds simple, but only a small part of the time that we spend online is actually devoted to business or retail. So you have to be smart and offer something different and have something inspiring to say. Not only that, but you need to make sure that mobile is at the heart of your digital strategy. Having a website that looks great on a desktop, but is messy on a mobile just won't cut it.

Millions of businesses exist in every corner of the world

Although it is very difficult to get complete figures, it is estimated that there are over 100 million companies in the world, but well under one million of those are large companies listed on stock markets around the world[25]. So most companies in all countries are small and medium-sized, with the vast majority of enterprises (between 70% and 95%) being micro-businesses[4]. Increasingly, in more and more economies, services account for a larger share, sometimes up to 80% of the economy.

What does this mean for your business?

It can actually be easier to get your company noticed in new countries, as the business landscape may not be as competitive and your website may be more impressive than the local competition. In addition, your products and services might be more in demand and you may even be able to identify a gap in the market that is not filled locally. You can then target those countries specifically, but make sure that information about your company, products and services can be found online in that region.

The shift online is from West to East

The world of business is changing dramatically, with there being a shift online from West to East. If you take a look at the top 20 most visited websites in the world today (according to Alexa's top site rankings[26]) you'll see companies that are recognised global names, including google.com, youtube.com, facebook.com, wikipedia.org, yahoo.com, amazon.com, twitter.com and instagram.com. But have you heard of any of the following names: baidu.com, google.co.in, qq.com, taobao.com, tmall.com, google.co.jp, vk.com and jd.com and weibo.com? These are household names in Asia and some of the most popular websites in the world. Baidu is the largest Chinese language search engine, while QQ is a hugely popular chat website. Taobao, Tmall and JD are huge online stores (the Chinese equivalent to eBay and Amazon) with hundreds of millions of customers. You've also got Indian and Japanese versions of Google appearing in this list, as well as the Russian social media network VKontakte. These are internet names that will be known in every household of the world in the future. But this is not a one-way street – competitors from other countries like China are already selling to your customers on Amazon in your country and targeting them with Google AdWords.

This is not just about brands from all over the world selling things to China, and it's also about Chinese companies selling their products to consumers all over the world.

Mike Evans, Alibaba president, interview with Bloomberg[27]

What does this mean for your business?

As the big technology players of the East spread their wings and expand globally, your business will find more digital tools at your disposal to reach customers all around the world. Searching on Baidu and listing on Tmall will become normal for you in the next few years. However, despite this massive opportunity, you will be faced with more competition from other businesses around the world, who you'll find playing in your backyard. So you need to get ahead of the curve now, so that you can compete with world-class companies, wherever they may be in the world, and overtake your competitors at home. It is a race you have to choose to run.

New technology platforms are springing up

The use of digital platforms has enabled 'unicorn' businesses, such as Uber and Airbnb, to build and expand quickly around the world, and rapidly rise to billion-dollar valuations.

Many of the digital services we use in our personal and business lives today were only invented in the last 20 years, yet we now depend on them every day. New, easy-to-use technology platforms and digital tools are available to quickly set up a business these days. There are tools you can use to build your own website, take payments online and easily communicate with customers at the click of a button, which have seriously changed the way that we do business all around the world. Some names you might recognise are WordPress, Shopify, PayPal, Stripe, Amazon, eBay, Facebook and Instagram.

> *In a recent survey of exporting SMEs, two out of three exporters stated that more than 50% of their international sales depended on online tools[28]. Furthermore, it is reported that small and medium-sized companies who have taken advantage of the internet bring in twice as much revenue than those who are not using it[29].*

What does this mean for your business?

There are exciting new ways to trade out there and the smartest businesses are always striving to adapt and make the most of these new technologies. You have to get into a digital mindset and be willing to incorporate new digital platforms and tools into the core of your business – not only to drive efficiencies, but also to build up an online relationship directly with customers all over the world. These platforms are already being used by millions of companies across the globe, so you must keep up and not get left behind.

Key Points

- ▶ The number of customers using the internet is absolutely booming, and most of them are connecting via mobile
- ▶ Potential customers and clients are literally everywhere around the world, and not necessarily where you would have first thought
- ▶ Competitors from the other side of the world are selling to your customers online
- ▶ Keep on changing and re-evaluating your business model and take advantage of technology platforms as the digital age marches on.

Resources

If you'd like more data on these disruptive trends, check out **www.growglobal.com/growfast.**

Chapter 2
The Digital Sales Channels

 With e-commerce there are no limits.

Helen Chapman, Founder, Dotty Fish

The good news is I'm keeping things simple. There are, in fact, only five widely used international digital sales channels that enable you to reach new customers around the world. To be successful, you need to select the best combination for your own products and services and then make them visible so they are in front of all your prospective customers.

In this chapter, I'm going to introduce you to these five key international digital sales platforms, their main features and some of the pros and cons of each in order to help you make a decision about the best options for your business and where to spend your digital budget.

But, first of all, how do you make the right choice?

The $5,000 Question

I'm often asked the question: "If I have a budget of $5,000 to grow my business globally, where should I invest it?"

Traditionally, this amount would be spent on attending an exhibition or trade fair in another country. It is surprising how quickly things add up once you factor in the preparation, the cost of the stand, the travel and accommodation expenses, the cost of follow-up, as well as the opportunity cost of being out of your business for a week.

But what if you were to invest it in digital instead?

Although many businesses are excited by the concept, they just don't know where to start. There are so many ways you could split the $5,000 budget, and so much hype and conflicting opinions about what is most important. Common battlegrounds include: investing in your website, posting on social media, listing on platforms such as Amazon, writing blogs or advertising on Facebook.

The ultimate question you need to ask is: **which one will get you more online leads or sales?**

Well, here is the answer.

There is a distinction between digital sales and digital marketing, with a lot of airtime dedicated to the latter, which often leaves the former forgotten. Having worked with literally hundreds of businesses in different sectors, I have seen time and time again there are two things you need to do. Your budget should ALWAYS be spent in this order as this system is fail-safe.

1. **You need to establish world-class digital sales platforms to allow you to earn revenue.**

2. **You need to implement successful digital marketing campaigns to drive traffic to those digital sales platforms.**

It may sound simple, but always get your digital sales platforms up to scratch before investing in digital marketing. There is no point paying for online advertising to send a lot of traffic to your website if, quite frankly, it is not really fit for purpose.

Digital Sales

Digital sales platforms are online places where a customer is able to purchase or express an interest in your products or services, whether you are selling to end customers or to other businesses. The needs of your business will be unique, but there are only really five popular digital sales channels to sell online to international customers that you can choose from:

- Through your own website
- Through an e-commerce website, taking payment online
- Through e-marketplaces, like Amazon and eBay
- Through s-commerce or social commerce, like Facebook and Instagram
- Selling through local partners, such as agents, distributors, retailers or stockists online.

If you're selling products, it is no longer just about selling through your website. A study[30] of retailers in the USA found that:

- 34% sell through their own website
- 25% sell through Facebook
- 16% sell through Amazon
- 22% sell through other marketplaces.

When making international online purchases, 46% of consumers do most or all of their shopping through marketplaces, compared to the 22% who do it through online retailers[22].

It is necessary for most companies to build more than one digital sales platform to create a fully effective balanced international digital strategy. This way you don't put all your eggs in one basket and are not beholden to the algorithms of just one of the internet giants, who can alter the fortunes of your business overnight.

I will take a look at each one in turn, so that you can weigh up the pros and cons of each for your business.

Website

Your website is your shop window. It's your primary channel to showcase your brand, products and services and get the message across clearly about your unique selling points, benefits and features, company history and ethos. A good website is the equivalent of being in a well-designed shop with helpful staff, whereas a poorly presented website is the equivalent of a jumble sale – it's hard for customers to find what they want, they feel that you don't really care about them and you haven't put any effort in. Ultimately, they will probably give up and click on to a competitor's site. A world-class website will attract visitors from all corners of the globe, and it is non-negotiable if you are serious about international growth. By world class, I mean a website that is well-optimised for search engines and ready for mobile devices, has an outstanding design and usability, and provides really top quality engaging content. It has to be technically robust with all of the online monitoring tools set up, so that you can evaluate the performance of your website as it is launched in new countries. Importantly, it should perform well and generate a good number of quality leads every month.

Where can you start?

Thankfully, new technology has made it much easier to build – with almost no technical skills at all – a well-designed and well-structured website on platforms like Squarespace, Weebly, Wix and Jimdo, as well as WordPress.com (the online version) or the web builder from a website hosting company, like GoDaddy or 1&1. Note there are two forms of WordPress: one is mainly just a hosted blogging platform where you don't need to download anything, and the other is a much more feature-rich version that you must download and host yourself. All these options are 'in the cloud' and offer attractive, customisable 'drag and drop' design templates, so they require no coding skills and allow you to build your website very quickly. You really can set up a website in a day and start for free on some of these platforms, although I would recommend that you use the business package for a low monthly fee of about $25, which provides you with added extras like website analytics, email and additional support.

Any of these digital platforms can be a good starting point if you have a new business or a very modest budget. They all have very similar features, so there is no real reason to choose one above the other. While they are being used more and more, they do have their limitations, so it can be tricky to add different languages, accept payment in different currencies and even get visibility in search engines around the world. Do be very careful when choosing your website platform in the first place. In fact, I would choose another option if you possibly can, if you have the time, budget and ambition to run an international business.

What are the international options?

Most businesses will need a more sophisticated website platform, with additional functionality to cater for international visitors and to scale internationally. I almost always suggest that my clients create their own WordPress website (the downloadable version that you host yourself). With over 50% of the world's websites being built in WordPress, it is a very popular choice[31, 32]. I suggest you use a website design and development agency or qualified freelancer to help you build a new WordPress website. The aim is to make sure your website is as world class as possible and to give you a solid technical foundation so that you can move forward and build a truly international website over time. This is a slightly more complex task to do yourself, but if you choose well, you'll be in the safe hands of your developer. Just a word of warning though: to build a WordPress website takes more time and more money. To build a well-structured, well-designed WordPress website with world-class content, may take up to a month to do, even if using a ready-made design template. Alongside the website build, you will have time to develop exceptional content, like images, text and videos.

The cost will depend on where in the world you get your website developed, and how much customisation and extra functionality you want. I find it typically costs between $500 and $5,000, but it is worth the investment as you end up with your own website as a digital sales platform that really reflects your brand and personality completely. In addition, you need to keep a website developer on a retainer to ensure that your new website is kept up-to-date and also make any changes you want to improve your website over time.

E-commerce

An e-commerce element on your website allows you to sell your products and services online directly to your customers. An e-commerce website brings in more money at a faster rate because it enables customers to buy immediately, 24 hours a day, 7 days a week. Through instant purchases, it stops them from going off to a competitor or losing interest while they wait to talk to you or get a reply to their email (especially if they are in a different time zone). It is also more profitable to sell through your own website, rather than through third-party partners who take a discount or commission, and cheaper for your business operations than face-to-face selling.

Increasingly, manufacturers are cutting out the intermediaries and selling directly to end customers through an e-commerce website, rather than going via distributors or other retail outlets. I have a manufacturing client whose product traditionally went through over five intermediaries, for historical reasons known only to them, who each shaved a cut off the margin, before it ended up in the end consumer's hands. You can imagine how much more profitable it was for them to start selling directly through their own website!

There are a few ways of doing this, but in essence, you need to set up an online product catalogue or services listing that is linked to basket or cart functionality with a checkout to take payments online.

It's not just traditional retail or manufacturing products that this works for. Services can also be sold like this, including online courses, translation services or professional audits.

Should you start small?

For international e-commerce, you need to be able to cater for international visitors buying in multiple currencies, using different payment methods, applying different sales tax, needing different delivery zones and methods, and speaking different languages, to name but a few international features.

For this reason, I wouldn't recommend using the online stores offered by the basic cloud web builders of the likes of Wix and GoDaddy. In my experience, businesses only get so far on these platforms before getting caught up in the limitations that prevent them from easily building a truly international e-commerce store with the international features that you will quickly want to add as your international customer base expands. One such case is Shopify, which is becoming increasingly popular. It is an excellent online shop at the forefront of domestic e-commerce that is perfect if you want to sell within your own country, or even sell across a region like Europe in euros. However, it is currently only built for a single currency at checkout, which makes things more limited, and it does not help you to internationalise your website[33]. There may be ways around this, but it adds unnecessary complexity, so I really recommend starting with a digital sales platform that is fully designed for international trade from the start.

Want to invest in international e-commerce?

If you are looking for an alternative that is easy to use, or you already have a basic WordPress company website, there are a selection of 'bolt-on' plug-in e-commerce modules that you can add to a WordPress website. The most popular of these by far is WooCommerce, which powers 28% of all online stores worldwide[34]. OpenCart is another option that should be on your shortlist of potential e-commerce platforms, as it is fairly straightforward to set up and use, although it does have to be structured for international customers in a very precise way.

You will normally need a web developer to help you set up and install the e-commerce functionality for both WooCommerce and OpenCart, but after that you'll be able to add your product and services yourself. I would recommend having a developer on-hand once it is built who can do routine updates of the software and tweaks as you develop your website still further. Adding e-commerce to your website will cost little more than just building a basic website, so put an initial budget of $1,000 to $5,000 aside to get started. Adding multiple languages and currencies will cost more, but you can do this in phases.

If you're looking for something a bit more heavy duty, then put Magento on your shortlist. It is much more complex, so you will definitely need a web developer with deep technical skills to build, configure and maintain it. Again, you will be able to add images and products and update the core pages yourself once the shell of your website is built. Whether this e-commerce website is going to be a significant part of your business and you plan to seriously invest in international e-commerce is your choice. This platform will allow you to have many integrations with other business systems, both in your organisation and outside of it, including complex customisations and personalisation. PrestaShop is widely used as an equivalent to Magento in some countries, like France and Spain, although Magento is much more widely used worldwide and has just been upgraded to a new all singing, all dancing version that is ready to take on the future of the digital age. These projects typically take about three months or more to complete, once quality content is put together, and I see clients paying from $5,000 to $50,000 or more for an e-commerce website, depending on their requirements, as well as where the website is developed and whether they use a freelancer of a certified agency.

Ready to sell without a website?

There are also ways of selling online without your own e-commerce website, particularly when it comes to selling services or selling to other businesses. This is where a third-party provider takes the payment on your behalf. You will need to look at the broadest definition of e-commerce, and not just limit it to a product-based online store. For example, your customers can pay their invoices online through your online accounting system (e.g. Xero), buy tickets to your events through an online booking website (e.g. Eventbrite) or book and pay for a consultation with you via an online calendar (e.g. Calendly).

E-marketplaces

An e-marketplace is essentially a virtual department store or mall, where you can list your products online on their store or platform. E-marketplaces also exist for digital products, services and expert skills. By adding your products and services to an online marketplace, you will get them in front of millions of customers who are already in purchasing mode and buying from a digital sales platform they trust. It is predicted that e-marketplaces will account for nearly 50% of all e-commerce worldwide in the next few years[12], with an incredible 85% of retail business in China already being done through these marketplaces[35]. In countries where there is a local Amazon, over 90% of customers shop at Amazon and 97% of people in China shop at Tmall[36]. That's nearly everyone. You are missing out if you are not using e-marketplaces. It's just important to select the right one.

Why use an e-marketplace rather than your own website?

You are effectively going straight to where customers already are, rather than having to attract them to come to you. In addition, you don't need to go to the effort of building and maintaining your own international e-commerce website, which can be time-consuming, costly and complex.

You simply need to create an account, upload your product or service descriptions, along with a way to collect payment, and you're good to sell. This can actually be done in an afternoon. From an international point of view, the best thing is these online selling platforms sell in the local currency and local language, often with local payment and local delivery methods, so you don't have to worry at all about this internationalisation. Typically, they provide all the checkout and payment functionality for you, including sales taxes, so once your products have been shipped or services delivered to the customer, you seamlessly get your payment transferred to your business bank account or digital wallet, minus any fees for listing on their platform.

While millions of businesses are already selling through online marketplaces in their home country, it is still quite a pioneering way to reach new customers in international markets. E-marketplaces are actually preferred in some regions, where people trust them more than a company's own website, particularly in China and Asia.

How do you know where to start?

Global e-marketplaces

Two of the most well-known global e-marketplaces are Amazon and eBay, and so they are a great place to test the water. They both have local versions, so in total, there are 14 Amazon sites around the world and 27 versions of eBay, such as Amazon France (amazon.fr) or eBay India (ebay.in).

However, there are also some other big online marketplaces expanding around the world from their original geographic hubs that are less well-known by some, including:

- Rakuten, the so-called 'Amazon of Japan'
- NewEgg, which focuses on electronics and tech and is embarking on a global expansion trail from the USA
- Mercado Libre, which spans out across Latin America, targeting Spanish and Portuguese speakers.

Country-specific e-marketplaces

If you've already got a country in mind, there are some big players in the largest e-commerce markets around the world to check out. Don't limit yourself to just the big global names, as these local online marketplaces have millions of customers themselves.

- In the US, the big offline retailers Sears and Walmart both have online marketplaces
- In China, Tmall, Taobao, JD, Xiu and Kaola are some of the biggest online marketplaces in the world selling billions of dollars of consumer goods
- In India, there are two major e-marketplaces, Flipkart and Snapdeal, which are becoming more and more popular
- In Southeast Asia, Lazada is growing as the internet population booms there.

Niche e-marketplaces

Aside from the giants listed above, there are literally hundreds more online marketplaces around the world that specialise in a specific product or service category. While some audiences may be smaller, you get the opportunity to target a much more targeted group of customers. You might not even have considered some of these as marketplaces, as you are using them every day.

Here are some examples of specialist online marketplaces to whet your appetite:

- Digital products have their own marketplaces e.g. iTunes for music, Amazon for e-books, Envato for website tools
- Services also can easily be sold via specialist marketplaces e.g. Amazon Services, Upwork for freelancers, Udemy for online courses
- B2B product can also be sold via e-marketplaces with a wider reach e.g. Alibaba, Amazon Business, NewEgg Business, IndiaMart

- Specialist niche B2C products can be sold on specific marketplaces e.g. NotOnTheHighStreet or Etsy for unique handcrafted gifts, Houzz for homewares, Polyvore or Zalando for fashion.

So, whatever you sell, there is an e-marketplace for you. In my work, I still see many companies who are very resistant to listing on online marketplaces as they say it detracts from and 'cheapens' their brand. The evidence is overwhelming that the future of e-commerce is through selling on e-marketplaces for most products and many services.

Online marketplace platforms can provide a quick and easy way to grow your international sales, but like everything else in life, think about all sides of the equation. A cautionary word though: it is not all plain sailing. Stringent application processes will apply to some product categories and online marketplaces, and you do need to work out your cross-border logistics, delivery, returns and customer support processes in advance. There are, of course, some costs of using e-marketplaces like listing, transaction and currency fees, which might mean they are not right for every business, especially if you have very low margin products or a high shipping cost. You are likely to get higher margins selling through your website, where you can foster a closer relationship with your customers than is possible on an online marketplace.

S-commerce

Selling your products through social media sites to customers around the world is a growing and much newer digital channel. This is known as social commerce, or s-commerce, and it is the integration of e-commerce functionality and online payment into social media networks. I'm not just talking about posting to social media here. Customers are still using social media as the best place to get inspiration for purchases, so it is, of course, important to do this. What I am describing here is taking things one step further, where the customer actually completes their purchase on, say, Facebook. The big global social media networks have been offering s-commerce since 2014, but most of them are still not yet open to all product types, all businesses or all countries worldwide (as they are mainly only accessible in the USA).

You may never have heard of s-commerce, so why should you consider it for your business?

Well, to start with, there is the opportunity to express your brand personality very easily, which is difficult in an online marketplace that is full of similar-looking product listings. S-commerce enables you to fully engage with your customers on the social media platform before they purchase, which helps enormously by building a relationship and trust. You also have the advantage of social proof, as potential customers can see if someone they know likes your brand or has purchased from you before, and look at testimonials from other happy customers. The quality of the customer and demographic information available from some social media websites, especially Facebook, is jaw-dropping and can be extremely targeted, which improves the quality and reduces the costs of your online advertising considerably (when you get it right).

Options for businesses selling consumer products through s-ecommerce on your business pages include a Facebook Shop, Buyable Pins on Pinterest and Shop Now on Instagram. The most incredible thing is that social media platforms are not currently charging you to sell through them at all. It is completely free and they take no listing fees or commission. In countries where these solutions have not been fully rolled out, you can often set up links directly back to products on your own e-commerce website, if you have one, for the customer to complete their purchase there.

Facebook has some neat lead generation techniques to pull in new clients worldwide, which are well suited if you are a service company or one that sells products to other businesses. LinkedIn does as well, if this social media platform is closer to your target demographic (although this is, of course, more 'digital marketing'). This is a great way to get leads, whether you are offering a spa treatment for holidaymakers or an initial free consultation if you are an architect or lawyer.

However, by far the biggest player in the field of social selling is WeChat in China, with nearly one billion users. You can set up a WeChat store very quickly, so that customers can shop with one click without leaving the app or going back to your local Chinese website to buy. It is predicted that China is three years ahead of the rest of the world in s-commerce[37], with 25% of people purchasing directly through a social channel already[19]. Companies in Europe and the United States, in particular, are lagging behind in their use of s-commerce.

Will s-commerce take over from websites and e-marketplaces?

Although the huge advantage of using s-commerce is that these social channels are free, the biggest downside is that customers are not usually in 'shopping' mode when they are on social media, so you are effectively interrupting them from their 'social' time. Having said that, it can be very effective for gift and impulse buys. I have seen small companies start by just setting up with a Facebook business page and shop, which takes only a few hours, as they make their first tentative steps into digital sales. They are often surprised at how far their shop reaches, as it brings in enquiries from the other side of the world.

As s-commerce is much more advanced in Asia, it is something to watch closely between now and 2020 as all the big social media companies roll out their s-commerce solutions globally. Now is a great time to experiment with social commerce, learn and get ahead of the curve.

Local Partners Online

One of the fastest and most tactical ways to sell more online and generate leads in other countries is to leverage the digital presence of your 'partners', whether they be agents, distributors, stockists, retailers or resellers. This can offer you a real shortcut to more international customers, because your partners will already have an established customer base in that region, a good reputation (if you chose well) and be able to nurture the customer relationship in the local language. They will also be aware of the local ways of doing business. This cuts out a lot of legwork, not to mention the costs involved in getting your business up to a similar level of operation and reputation in another country.

How should you start?

To get started, you just need to get your products or services featured prominently on your partners' websites. You can do this by giving them good quality content about your products and services in terms of text, images and videos, which is well-optimised for search engine visibility. Keep the text clear and simple, so that people who speak English as a second or third language can understand it or it can be easily translated.

It is also important to select partners who are digital savvy. In most cases, they already have a website or e-commerce website, which is listed and established in their country's search engines. You can check how good your distributor or retailer is online by looking at both their website and their positioning in the local search engine, then carrying out a test of their web rank on Alexa Web Ranking or Similar Web. If they are not as sophisticated web-wise as you, you might want to offer them training and suggest that they upgrade their existing website and social media to attract more online leads and sales. They may also be able to manage e-marketplace listings for you.

Why work closely with your partners?

If you want to take working with your partners one step further, you can develop a 'website in a box', which is a simple version of your site that can be adapted by your partners for that country's customers. It can be quickly launched by your local partner as a local website with products or services that will appeal to local customers and in the local language. Make sure that you register all your local website domain names yourself upfront and retain all the intellectual property rights, then license the use of them to your partner. This approach will give you both more control over your brand and the flexibility to change partner in the future if things don't work out as planned.

Having a local partner can jump you over quite a few expensive and time-consuming obstacles. However, you obviously pay a price for this service, which can either be a commission or selling your products to them at a much lower cost in the first place. You will also need to spend time maintaining a good working relationship with them. As with online marketplaces, you won't get full customer data or even know who your end customers are a lot of the time. Plus, without good training, your partners might not represent your brand story correctly.

Think carefully about your overall international digital strategy and the selling rights that you give your partners, as you can often end up directly competing with your local partners online if you do decide to sell into that country via a different digital sales channel at a later date.

Key Points

▸ Your sales and marketing budget can literally go a long way if you invest in digital to gain new international customers

▸ There is a distinction between digital sales and digital marketing — build your world-class digital sales platforms first, then do the digital marketing

▸ Define a set budget to invest in things that will directly increase online leads and sales as a priority

▸ There are only five popular digital sales platforms you can build: a website, e-commerce website, e-marketplaces, s-commerce and selling online through partners in other countries

▸ It is critical to choose the right combination of digital sales platforms for your products and services, so take into account your budget and longer-term digital and international ambitions.

Resources

If you'd like more advice on which digital sales channel to choose or how to build a world-class digital sales channel, check out the bonus content on **www.growglobal. com/growfast** and download my Digital Sales Channel Comparison Table.

Chapter 3
Digital Visibility Around The World

 With 1.8 billion websites, if you publish a website it is very unlikely it will get noticed... Unless you are prepared to produce quality content, perform Search Engine Optimisation (SEO) and spend on marketing. Or you may get lucky, and be the next big thing, as all the top sites were once.

How many websites are there in the world? Tek Eye[38]

The digital world is so busy these days with so much 'noise' around, it's really hard to get noticed and stand out. To reach these millions of potential customers and attract the right ones, you need to make yourself visible online to your particular niche target market. You've really got to take this seriously to be in the game and both survive and thrive in this digital age. If your customers can't find you online, they won't know about you, and how can they get information about your products and services and buy from you if they don't know about you?

In this chapter, I'm going to show you where you need to be visible in front of your online customers around the world, so that you can sell to them, and how this differs in different countries around the world. With an understanding of the options that are open to you, you can assess where to focus your efforts for your particular business.

Are you visible in this international digital world?

It used to be enough for your website to appear in the first three pages of a search engine, which was quite easily achieved by adding a few relevant words to your website pages. When Google was founded in September 1998, it was serving just ten thousand search queries per day, but now every day Google is answering more than 4 billion questions from people around the globe in 181 countries and 146 languages[39]. Things have moved on considerably, and the digital world has become much more complex, with so many more digital sales, marketing platforms and tools at your disposal.

What is more, it is also more competitive. You are now competing with more and more companies from around the world, who you probably didn't even consider as competitors before. They are targeting your customers at home, on your home turf, through online channels. For example, you can now purchase a product from a Chinese seller on amazon.co.uk at a very good price and it will arrive the next day.

Do you know what you're up against?

Despite the massive opportunity out there, many companies are invisible on the web. Your company could easily get lost amongst all the search engines with millions of website listings, and on e-marketplaces where there are millions of products for sale or on social media platforms that have billions of posts, all competing for attention.

Here's food for thought and some figures from 2017 to show how competitive the digital world is[38, 39, 40, 41]:

- 170 million active sites were recorded
- Less than 1 million websites (0.1%) accounted for over 50% of web traffic
- Only 10% of all websites were updated regularly
- Over 99% of websites got almost no traffic

- Amazon had over half a billion products listed worldwide
- eBay had over 1 billion products listed
- Facebook had over 2 billion users
- YouTube had over 1.5 billion users
- Instagram was approaching 1 billion users.

The opportunity is definitely there, but you need to have a reality check. You need to make sure you are truly world class and stand out online in all the places where people are spending their time before you can grow globally. With so much competition out there, it will take strategy, planning and investment, in both time and money, to take advantage of this opportunity. Whichever digital sales channel you select, you will need to both distinguish and optimise it, as you need to have a great brand, outstanding design and top engaging content that it is technically optimised for search engines and mobile devices.

Before you delve in, remember it is really important to make sure that your digital sales platforms are completely world class, before you start putting too much money into getting visible.

Search Engines Around The World

When it comes to gaining international visibility online, your first job will be to ensure your own website is optimised for international sales and appears in search engines around the world. Someone told me the other day that 'having a website that has not been optimised, is like having a movie that has never been screened'. The same goes for your other digital sales channels too – whether it be your e-commerce store, your online marketplaces listings or your social media shops.

Google

If you look at how the web works around the world, Google dominates as the leading global search engine with a market share of over 90% in all countries[42], except China and Russia. But when I say the majority of people worldwide use Google, I don't mean they are just searching on google.com. They are actually searching on their local version of Google, as that is where Google will send them. So, if you are searching in the UK, you are directed to google.co.uk, in Australia it is google.com.au., and in France you're directed to google.fr in French, and so on. There are nearly 200 local versions of Google, and many of these local versions are available in multiple languages too: google.co.in in India has 10 languages and google.co.za in South Africa has seven languages. There are many more bilingual versions of Google, like google.ca in Canada, which is available in both French and English.

It is critical to appreciate that Google is available in all these different country and language versions because Google will only serve you up your local country version of its search engine. Therefore, see it as a subset of all the information that it holds for the whole world. When I used to look for a local restaurant in my hometown of Brighton UK by searching for 'fish restaurant Brighton', I used to get results for Brighton in Melbourne, Australia and Brighton in New York, USA. That clearly doesn't happen anymore and hasn't for a very long time. Essentially, any search engine wants to be able to present the most relevant search results, depending on the country you are searching from and the language you're speaking (including British English, American English and Australian English!). They are looking for two things: web pages with content that targets customers in a particular country and pages in a customers' local language.

Your challenge is to make sure that your website, marketplace listing or social media shop appears in the right country version of Google, in the right language.

If you only have a .co.uk website in English, it may do well on google.co.uk, but it won't necessarily do so well on any other local version of Google. If you want to sell to customers online in Australia, you will need to do well on google.com.au, as that is where potential Australian customers will be searching. Likewise, if you want to sell to customers in France, you need good local targeted website content in French that is doing well in google.fr. For example, if you have a page on your website in French on a French website domain like abc.fr, then it is likely to appear more prominently in the French Google than an English page on abc.co.uk would do.

Beyond Google

Don't forget that there are other search engines in other parts of the world that are well used, apart from Google. Yahoo! and Bing tend to have below a 5% share in most countries around the world, but a bigger 11% of market share of search in the USA. The two big exceptions are Baidu in China and Yandex in Russia.

Baidu is the leader in China with over two-thirds of the search engine market share, particularly as Google is not available in China (although it is in Hong Kong). China also has other emerging search engines too, such as Shenma, which has just under a 20% market share dedicated to mobile search, while others, including Haosou and Sogou, have less than a 10% market share.

In Russia, Yandex and Google are running circles around each other, with just over 50% and 40% of the search market share respectively. Yandex is becoming a regional search engine, gaining users in other countries with large numbers of Russian speakers, where it has between a 10% and 30% market share in countries such as Belarus and Kazakhstan.

There are also some country-specific search engines that are popular, including Naver (in South Korea, which has about a 25%

share), Daum (in South Korea with a 7% share), Seznam (Czech Republic with a 15% share) and Yahoo! Japan (which has more than a 25% share of the search market there). But even in these markets, users have generally moved to the local version of Google over the past five years[42].

Beyond search engines

The lines are blurring as to what a search engine actually is, because your customers are searching in other online places and spaces. You could say that Amazon is the search engine for products (many shoppers look to Amazon first, even before Google), Wikipedia is the search engine for facts, and YouTube is the search engine for videos. So, if your products aren't listed on Amazon and you don't have a company video on YouTube, then you are not going to be as visible as you could be.

Where should you be visible?

While I can't say that it is all about Google, internationally speaking, it mostly is. So you need to make sure your company, brand, products and services are visible on:

- All of the local versions of Google, where you would like to do business
- The big international search engines, like Baidu and Yandex, if you are doing business in Chinese or Russian
- Any relevant local search engine if you are going to be doing business there
- Alternative 'search engines', like Amazon or YouTube.

E-Marketplaces Around The World

Millions of people are buying millions of products and hundreds of businesses are procuring services across the globe through online marketplaces, so make sure that you get a piece of the action.

When it comes to getting your product or services listings visible in front of customers all over the world, it is crucial that you are seen both on the local version of the search engine and the right online marketplace.

There are three elements to the online marketplace visibility challenge:

- Choosing the right marketplaces where your customers are already spending time (so that your products and services are more likely to found by the right people)

- Making sure your products or services stand out among the hundreds of competing listings in that marketplace (don't forget how many others will be listing similar offerings on the same platform)

- Setting up for selling to international customers so that you can ship across the world.

Are you on the right version of the e-marketplace?

Given that there are many local versions of online marketplaces around the world that target different countries and speakers of different languages, you need to make sure you are listing on the right version. In the case of the local versions of Amazon and eBay, for example, if you search in google.fr in France in French, you will see amazon.fr or ebay.fr, and if you search in google.co.in in India in English, you are likely to see amazon.in or ebay.in.

It is the same with many other online marketplaces too, like Mercado Libre in Latin America: mercadolibre.com.ar appears on the Argentinian version of Google and mercadolivre.com.br appears on Google Brazil (note the difference in spelling changes from *libre* in Spanish to *livre* in Portuguese). Rakuten operates in over 25 countries worldwide too. There are local websites, like rakuten.co.jp, which you will see if you are searching in Japan, but you are more likely to see its global site – global.rakuten.com – in other countries around the world.

If you just want to be visible in front of customers in China, or on Baidu specifically, then it makes sense for you to be listing on Tmall, for example. The same applies to all the local and specialist online marketplaces, whether they be IndiaMart or Zalando. Go for the online marketplace that best reflects both your customer type and the country where they live and work.

Does your listing really stand out?

The challenge is to make sure your listing is irresistible to your niche audience, that the description is optimised and any messaging in your advertising spot-on. Being on these crowded marketplaces is not enough in itself, you need to make sure that your listings are better than your competitors.

This entails a very similar approach to getting visibility in search engines: you need to optimise your listings correctly with good product or service descriptions and images, and add relevant search terms in all the right places. To increase your visibility and boost sales even more, it is becoming increasingly necessary to pay for online promotion within the platform. This way you will get noticed by using your ad spend to convert browsers into buyers before your competitors do.

You must also translate your listings into the local language and localise your product descriptions for the local market. For example, is there a product in your range that is preferred by customers from a specific country? If so, make sure you list that first.

Essentially, don't just list on, say, amazon.co.uk in English, as it won't work and guarantee you visibility around the world, as it won't get you in front of the right customers in the right countries. I've seen lots of well-meaning businesses fall for this common mistake, but it's a shortsighted approach. You need to take the time to treat each market individually and optimise your offerings for that country or specific marketplace or you'll be throwing away a secret key to unstoppable international growth.

Are you set up to ship around the world?

Finally, think about your logistics. All the largest online marketplaces, including Amazon and eBay, have established programmes for international selling that allow your products to be listed on their different country websites and shipped worldwide, sometimes by simply clicking a single button. Some e-marketplaces also help with global shipping too, which takes a lot of the stress out of getting your products from one side of the world to another. All you have to do is send them to a local depot in your home country for the online marketplace to bulk ship onwards to the destination country. While this service is not available to all businesses in all countries yet, my prediction is that this will become easier and easier to do as the online marketplaces encourage increasing numbers of overseas companies to join their ranks.

Where should you be visible?

To recap, you need to make sure your products and services are listed and visible on:

- All of the local versions of Amazon, eBay, Rakuten and Mercado Libre, where you would like to do business
- The big online marketplaces, like Tmall and JD, if you want to reach Chinese customers

- Any specialised e-marketplace by country or sector e.g. Lazada for South East Asia or Zalando for fashion in Europe
- Any other sector-specific online marketplace e.g. UpWork, iTunes, Alibaba or IndiaMart, depending on your product or service.

Social Media Around The World

With more than 3 billion people using social media every month, mostly through their mobiles, social media is big in practically every country around the world and it's growing at a rate of over 1 million a day[19]. Imagine the potential you have to connect with and sell to new potential customers across the world.

The Big 7

It is an amazing statistic that if Facebook was a country, its population would be the largest in the world – larger than China (1.4 billion) and India (1.3 billion) with over 2 billion users! It is closely followed by YouTube with nearly 1.5 billion users a month, and then Instagram with 800 million average monthly users, which is much higher than the whole population of the next biggest country, the USA, at 324 million. Interestingly, some of the social media networks we hear about every day are mere minnows in the global social network world: Twitter (330 million), Google+ (300 million), LinkedIn (260 million) and Pinterest (200 million)[19].

All the global social media networks have millions of users across the world and are available in many languages, so you can communicate with and sell to your customers in different countries speaking different languages. Facebook is available in over 90 languages and LinkedIn has members in 200 countries and territories around the globe. It is available in 24 languages and is the leading business social media network.

The big story of 2017 has been the phenomenal rise in the use of chat apps, like WhatsApp and Facebook Messenger, that both have around 1.5 billion users. Skype, Snapchat and Viber have around 200-300 million users each worldwide[19].

Local social media platforms

Beyond the big players, there are a whole host of popular local social networking sites available in different countries that you probably wouldn't have heard of unless you'd actually done business there.

In Europe, there is XING, which is a professional social networking site that's a bit like LinkedIn and used a lot for recruitment. It is popular in German-speaking countries like Germany, Austria and Switzerland. Viadeo is another professional social network that is popular in French-speaking and Spanish-speaking countries.

In Russia, VK (originally VKontakte) is similar to Facebook and the largest European social network with nearly 100 million users. It is popular amongst Russian speakers and the second most visited site in Russia. Then there is Odnoklassniki, a social network service for classmates and old friends, which is a bit like the UK's Friends Reunited (if you can remember that!).

After our world tour of social media sites, we come to China, where the social media landscape is very different. This is mainly because some of the big global social media names I have just mentioned are not present. Have you heard of the Great Firewall of China? Well, China has some giant 'homegrown' social media networks because of this. The one exception to this rule is LinkedIn, which is available in China, in association with local Chinese partners.

Sina Weibo is a Chinese micro-blogging service for Mandarin and Cantonese speakers, similar to Twitter, which has nearly 400 million users. It's also used in other Chinese speaking countries, like Taiwan. It is incredibly popular, being one of the most used sites in China.

YouKu is China's biggest video site and is widely used instead of YouTube, with a new arrival, called YY, which is a video-based social network. Qzone is one of the original Chinese social networking websites, now with over 500 million users. Needless to say, chat apps are much more widely used than social media sites in China, with WeChat and QQ being the largest. They both are approaching 1 billion monthly active users.

Outside of China, the general trend is for users to migrate to the larger, more global social media networks that you all know and love, as they can be accessed in more and more languages[43]. However, there are still rare occasions when these are closed down by national governments for political, security and regulatory reasons. So, if you feel that social media is absolutely key to your business success, you might want to build a presence and following on a local social media network in a particular country too, just in case.

Where should you be visible?

To be visible on social media, you need the most enticing and engaging content, tailored to a local market and in local languages. As it is so difficult to get visibility, I recommend almost routinely that you pay for online ads on the social media networks, which can be surprisingly low cost, starting from, say, $5 a day.

Again, which of the social media networks you need to be visible on will depend on if you are selling to consumers or other businesses, and which country you are doing business in. In general:

- Set up business pages on Facebook and Instagram if you're connecting to customers and want a global reach
- Try LinkedIn and Twitter if you're selling to other businesses
- Go for YouTube whoever you are selling to or whatever you're selling, as video is where it is now at, and make sure you go live on Facebook regularly
- Keep an eye out for local social media networks in different countries that appeal to speakers of different languages, like Xing and Viadeo
- Tackle the big social media networks and chat platforms, like WeChat, QQ, YouKu and VK, if you are doing business in Chinese or Russian
- Get ahead of the curve by adding shop functionality to your social media and chat business pages, like a Facebook shop or a WeChat store to sell.

Avoid Digital Invisibility

I cannot stress how important being visible online is. Most companies I work with are invisible to their target customers online around the world.

You need to have web pages, e-marketplace listings or social media stores with localised content in the local language that is targeted to a particular country to help you be visible on these local versions of the search engines.

As with all international digital sales channels, you really do need to make sure that you are adapting your content to optimise it for international customers, and not just focusing on one country or thinking that what worked on one digital sales channel in one country can be copied and replicated in exactly the same way for another country with the same results.

The digital world is global – seize the opportunity!

Key Points

▸ The digital world is crowded and noisy, so you must stand out and be visible

▸ Set up your business so that it is visible online to customers in different countries, speaking different languages

▸ Make your chosen digital sales platform as world class as it can possibly be, then distinguish it and optimise it

▸ Make sure you are visible on the big global digital platforms, but don't forget to give the smaller or local platforms a go too

▸ It is likely you will have to pay for online advertising these days to get to the level of visibility that you need across the digital world.

Resources

If you'd like to find out more about getting visible, check out **www.growglobal.com/growfast** for bonus content. You can download a Reading List, as well as take the Digital Invisibility Test.

SEIZE THE OPPORTUNITY.
ARE YOU READY TO START?

Digital technologies are improving prospects for small businesses... to participate in global trade. They enable enterprises to cut costs, streamline supply chains, and market products and services worldwide with greater ease than before.

Information Economy Report 2017, United Nations
Conference on Trade and Development (UNCTAD)[1]

Now you know the theory, it's time to take action and meet those international customers who are ready and waiting to buy from you! You are going to have to make a lot of big decisions if you want fast global growth. It's exciting and it can be tempting to rush in, but you need to carefully select the right countries to sell into and the right digital channels to use.

Do you want to grow internationally without having to invest in setting up overseas offices, or go on expensive trade missions and exhibitions, or have a difficult-to-manage sales team on the ground? Do you want an easy way to specifically target the right customers online? Or do you need to kick-start your international revenue? Let me show you how it's done...

In Part B, I'm going to clearly lay out the international digital journey that every company goes through on the quest for international online growth and the 6 steps of my fail-safe Grow Global Method. This is a unique system I have crafted over 10 years of working closely with over 700 companies, and having helped thousands more through webinars, seminars and workshops. It gets results fast, and can definitely help to grow your business internationally. This 6-step system will save you time and resources by teaching you exactly what you need to focus on, so that you do the right things in the right order. So many businesses flounder due to lack of direction and a haphazard trial and error approach. You can cut straight to the chase by building a solid strategy to action, point by point. I'll also give you some practical hints and tips about what exactly you need to consider for your particular business type.

Are you ready to seize the international digital opportunity before your competitors do?

Chapter 4
The International Digital Journey

During my work with hundreds and hundreds of companies, I have observed that every business goes through the same journey when preparing to sell online internationally. I've seen some companies take over 10 years to go through it, while others have done it within a year. I have a client who came to a seminar with me in 2008 and only started to update her website in 2016, with a view to generating leads and selling online to international customers in the future. Imagine all the sales she has lost over those 8 years – it breaks my heart! Another client came to me with a very good e-commerce website that was generating hundreds of thousands of pounds in online sales in the UK. They decided to launch their US website straight away, and within a year it had matched their UK site for sales, getting hundreds of thousands of pounds in dollars. That's fast progress!

In this chapter, I'm going to show you the typical path a company takes when negotiating the journey to more international online sales. You will be able to recognise where you are and get yourself ready to move forward to the next stage.

I have looked at many companies who have succeeded and what they have done well. Generally, it comes down to being able to make swift, steady progress through these 8 key stages. I've also looked at companies who have not achieved the results they expected and the mistakes they have made. These often come down to inaction, doing things on the cheap and missing growth opportunities.

Using the Grow Global Method (explained in the next chapter), you can minimise the time you spend on each of the stages, and even leapfrog over a couple, so that you can start selling in as many countries as possible through different digital sales channels in the fastest time possible.

Can you identify where you are on your international digital journey now?

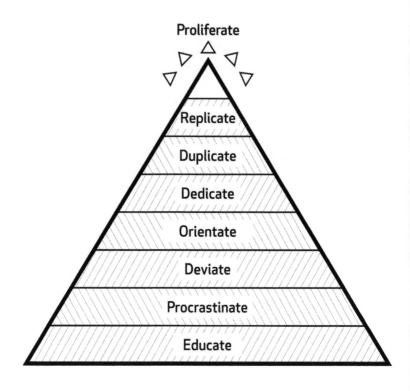

Stage 1: Educate

At this stage, you have a good business in your own country, but you've not thought about making more of digital to grow your business. Essentially, you've not thought about selling to customers in other countries either. Actually, you are sceptical about all things international or digital.

If you are in the **Educate** stage, it is likely that:

- You are totally unaware that you would benefit from going international or digital. In the UK, for example, under 20% of all companies export or work internationally, when up to 80% could do so

- You are aware some of your competitors are selling online around the world, but think it is just something that other people do and don't realise it is an opportunity within your reach

- You have an old-fashioned website that doesn't really work for you

- You're not bothered with social media or the likes of Amazon and eBay, as you think they are a waste of time

- You lack the skills or know-how in your company to take on the challenge of digital global growth

- You ignore any emails or enquiries that come in from overseas, thinking they are spam

- You are worried about selling online because of credit card fraud.

Challenges: You are being held back by your mindset and are totally missing the opportunity and additional revenue that selling online internationally can bring to your business. Worse still, your competitors are likely to be communicating with all your potential customers and may even start capturing their attention and take them away from you.

Stage 2: Procrastinate

At this stage, you know that you should use digital to go international and are aware of the opportunity, but you've not yet started doing it.

If you are in the **Procrastinate** stage, it is likely that:

- You know you need to be investing in digital, but you have never quite get around to it. It stays on the to-do list as it is all so complicated and you don't know where to start, so something else is always a higher priority

- You're still relying on your traditional sales channels, as you've always done, going to international exhibitions and sending out catalogues and brochures

- Your traditional sales channels may no longer be working for you, making your business struggle as your stockists and distributors are not hitting the sales targets that you'd agreed

- You may also think that your company is just too small to take on the challenge of global growth

- You don't realise that you'll be left behind if you fail to take advantage of digital.

Challenges: You are so put off by all the work and effort involved in achieving global growth you are not even off the starting block. You have lost sight of the opportunity. Of course, everyone is busy with limited time and resources, but the world is changing around you at a very fast pace. So, by not embracing the digital and international arenas, you continue to throw away potential revenue year on year.

Stage 3: Deviate

At this stage, you finally decide that you are going to start looking into this digital thing, but feel that if you have to do it, then you are going to do it as cheaply as possible and in your spare time. You don't give it the proper resources it needs.

If you are in the **Deviate** stage, it is likely that:

- You are only putting a small budget and the minimum of effort into international and digital and really paying 'lip service' to it, carrying out lacklustre experiments on the fringes

- You are starting to half-heartedly update your website, but it is a false start, as you are on the wrong tracks and the wrong platform, not working to best practice

- If you hire some help for your website, you are use a freelancer who doesn't charge much and may be your sister's boyfriend's best friend's next-door neighbour. They are so cheap that you think you can't go wrong. But they will only do what you tell them to do, and you're not really sure what you should be telling them to do in the first place.

Challenges: This stage may be clumsy, but at least it's a start, even if you are going around in circles and taking one step forward and two steps backwards. Despite this haphazard approach, you might even get a few enquiries or sales through your website.

Stage 4: Orientate

At this stage, you regroup and start to take digital seriously, and start to make small changes and begin to see the results (despite the inevitable element of trial and error). By now you are convinced there must be something in this digital approach, so it must be worth investing more time in it.

If you are in the **Orientate** stage, it is likely that:

- You find a new, reliable website developer or agency
- You write a plan for the changes you want to make to your website to make it world class
- You move to a new best practice website platform or update the design of your existing website
- You put your web company on a retainer
- You start to consistently generate a few leads or sales from the website every month and even had one from another country last month, almost by accident.

Challenges: You start to see what is possible and make good progress for a few months. Things then plateau out and you feel you can't get any further. You need to step things up as your competitors are snapping at your heels.

Stage 5: Dedicate

At this stage, you really embrace digital and make it a core part of your business. Things are getting exciting now. Your website starts to perform, delivering significant quality leads or online sales each and every month. You now feel you cannot survive and grow your business without embracing digital strategies.

If you are in the **Dedicate** stage, it is likely that:

- You invest in digital as an alternative sales and marketing channel
- You go back to first principles and check that every part of your digital platform and infrastructure is implemented as well as it can be to build a solid foundation for your digital strategy
- You relaunch your website, so that it is on a leading platform, is truly world class and is built to best practice, ready for international visitors

- You bring a full-time team member in to manage your digital platforms
- You build a full digital strategy and plan for your business, ticking off tasks every month
- You check your website and online marketplace reports every morning to a stream of leads and sales
- Digital is making a good contribution of over 20% to your overall revenue
- You are even getting a few international orders coming in through your website.

Challenges: At this stage, you are starting to get into the zone. Sometimes, it does feel that everything is taking much longer than you'd like it too, but with every new improvement you make, you are rewarded with increased leads and sales. You start to wonder where you should go next.

Stage 6: Duplicate

Now you select one new country where you'd like to do more business and start to investigate how to reach and appeal to more customers there. At this stage, things are paying off.

If you are in the **Duplicate** stage, it is likely that:

- You set up your website in your first international market, like the USA, by duplicating your successful online offering from your home country. For example, taking your UK website and creating a US version
- Revenue starts to build and you are getting as many sales from your new country as you are getting from your own country
- You do the same with your e-marketplace listings, like extending your UK product listings from amazon.co.uk to amazon.com.

Challenges: You probably find this international stuff complex and confusing as you go into a new country for the first time. You learn that each country has its own ways of doing things and so needs to be treated differently. There's so much to think about adjusting, from pricing to sales tax. You're worried that you're not on the right track, but bit-by-bit you get to grips with everything by researching, trying new things and asking for help.

Stage 7: Replicate

At this stage, you are now confident that you can grow your business online in other countries around the world and have a priority list of countries to enter from your market research. You now have the skills in the business to replicate your website, online marketplaces and social commerce shops so that you can trade in new countries, along with an ever-improving process to follow.

If you are in the **Replicate** stage, it is likely that:

- You are carefully working your way through a plan, adding a couple of new countries every year
- You find it easier and easier each time you go into a new country, as you know what you're looking for and building on experience from the last country
- You see revenue grow from every new market – you may even double your online sales year on year as you bring on more and more countries
- You stop using international stockists and distributors in favour of doing things directly online.

Challenges: You are now growing so fast you face the dilemma of when to recruit new team members in all areas of your business, and you also need to make sure that you are hiring the very best.

Stage 8: Proliferate

At this stage, you are now focused on driving growth across multiple digital sales channels and multiple countries. Now, over half your business is selling to international customers online.

If you are in the **Proliferate** stage, it is likely that:

- You pull together a full international digital strategy and have a defined process to expand and monitor the progress
- You plan to sell online in other ways, like online marketplaces or selling through social media in other countries
- You have plans to grow your online business 100% year on year
- You can enter three or more new countries each year
- You have a great internal team, with someone responsible for digital and a great team of reliable world-leading digital suppliers.

Challenges: None! You are in the zone and on the journey to unstoppable international growth!

How can you move up the international digital journey fast?

If you honestly want to expand your business internationally, then the first step is to acknowledge where you are on the journey. Ask yourself how quickly you want to move along the international journey. If you're starting out, my Grow Global Method will take you through step by step what you need to do to get started. My dream would be for you to start straight away at the **Orientate** stage after reading this book (so ticking off the **Educate** stage). This is so you can avoid the pain of the **Procrastinate** and **Deviate** stages and reap the rewards of more online international sales sooner, as you swiftly move to **Dedicate**, **Duplicate**, **Replicate** and **Proliferate**, which is where your business needs to be in this digital age.

Interview with Cressida Granger, Managing Director of Mathmos

www.mathmos.com

The company was founded over 50 years ago by Edward Craven Walker, the inventor of the original lava lamp and is now an iconic British heritage product, sold around the world, featuring in famous TV shows, like Dr Who and The Prisoner and owned by celebrities. We are the best in the world and we just work to get that message across. We focus on making sure our product is great as there is no place to hide with online reviews.

We used digital really early on and even won a Design Week award for our website in 1997 – pre-Google! At this point, we were not selling online, just brand building. We were early to e-commerce and as soon as it became feasible to sell online, we did. It wasn't huge volumes to start with.

But we got to the point where we decided to dedicate to digital in about 2012 and our website has served us really well. It then took years to make the transition and move the business towards this online vision, as we had been selling through more traditional wholesalers and stockists beforehand and needed to wind down this side of the business.

We experimented with different product ranges online, driven mostly by our wholesalers wanting a much fuller range. It diluted our heritage by broadening our range to keep the wholesalers happy. So now we have moved back to having just one range. For us online, it's all about search. In our case it's about 'lava lamp' - niche marketing is easier.

We've sold internationally from the very beginning as we knew that the UK was a small market. Really it is as easy to sell abroad, as it is to sell to Birmingham. And going international is fun!

Europe is a tough market as you have to deal with different languages and different cultures – the French are very different customers to the Germans for example, and you have to take different customer preferences into account.

We've got our main mathmos.com website and then we've three established local websites for France, Germany and Spain, where demand is highest. We've then built new websites for the Netherlands, Switzerland, Denmark and Sweden. Absolutely everything is translated on these websites and adapted for customers in those countries, including putting them into euros, adding payment methods that are popular in those countries, as well as about updating the terms and conditions of sale, which we've added bit by bit over a few years.

We sell on Amazon in five countries around Europe, including the UK, France, Germany, Italy and Spain and run Amazon advertising to help with our sales. We've listings on eBay in the UK and Germany and Facebook shops.

Everything is built upon a systemised business and processes, so I trust my team to run with it and we're continually improving everything month on month. Over time, I've had to upskill the team to work in the digital world and I envision that I'll have to keep on doing that. We keep researching our markets as they are forever changing, evolving and reskilling as the digital landscape changes every year.

Key Points

- ▶ There are 8 distinct stages every company travels through on their international digital journey

- ▶ These are: **Educate, Procrastinate, Deviate, Orientate, Dedicate, Duplicate, Replicate** and **Proliferate**

- ▶ Move through the stages as quickly as possible by following the Grow Global Method and skipping the **Procrastinate** and **Deviate** stages altogether

- ▶ Get ahead and then keep ahead of your competitors.

Resources

If you'd like to find out where you are on your international digital journey, check out **www.growglobal.com/growfast** for bonus content and to download the International Digital Journey Template.

Chapter 5
The Grow Global 6-Step Method

Now that you know the typical journey that a business takes on the path to international digital success, you need to plot your own steps to transform your company and achieve unstoppable international growth. To be successful, you will need to follow a proven path. As with many things in business and in life, if you approach it in the right way from the outset, you will achieve your goal more quickly and efficiently.

In this chapter, I am going to reveal my fail-safe 6-step method to deliver serious international growth to your business by showing you what you need to do to expand into more and more countries by using digital channels. I'm passionate about helping businesses to fulfil their international potential, and have created this step-by-step system to ensure that you can safely enter a new international market and win more international online leads and sales. My prescriptive method will save you time, money and get you growing your business in the right way from day 1, at a lot lower risk.

It's a bit like when I was training for my first 5k run. As I jogged around the park a couple of times, I was getting a bit fitter and going a bit further each day. After about a week, I started to give up, slow down and walk more and more. So I decided to download the training schedule from the website, which told me exactly which days to run on, how long to run for, how far to go and when to take a rest day. I made much better progress and found it so much easier to keep going because I was following a plan that thousands of others had followed successfully, without having to worry if I was doing the right things or not. Within a week, I was running 1k without stopping. The second week, it was 2k, the third week 3k and by the end of the month, I went for the whole 5k. I was so excited to have made so much progress so quickly. The next year, I hired a personal trainer who adapted the downloaded schedule for my health and fitness level, as well as giving me additional advice on nutrition and hydration. He was there to keep me motivated and on track, and also answered my questions. My fitness peaked so quickly, I decided to double my challenge and enter a 10k race! All this extra help has meant that I now also know how to live a healthy fit life every single day.

Using the Grow Global Method is exactly the same. If you dip in and out of the bits you like, you'll definitely make some progress, but not nearly enough (you'll play it safe).

If you follow the advice in this book, you'll make good steady progress and start to increase your international online sales (you'll grow at pace). If you're just starting, then go through every step in sequence. If you're already selling online internationally, use the checklists in the method to see if you've covered off everything as well as you possibly can.

With me on hand as your personal trainer, you can get to your end goal much faster. You can even win the race by joining one of my transformation programmes, which are drawn from the success of hundreds of companies who have gone before you.

How you implement the Grow Global Method is up to you. It depends on how fast you want to grow globally.

Let's see what you can achieve!

Introduction to the 6 Steps

My method is not reliant on any clever digital marketing or SEO tricks. It is simply about first building a successful online business in your home country, and then replicating that success in other countries around the world. **Copy, paste, adjust.**

It doesn't matter if you're selling services or products, as long as you are selling something that is unique or can be differentiated.

This method applies to the largest enterprise or the smallest start-up. It can be adopted whether you are selling to customers (B2C) or to other businesses (B2B) (or both). This method works for everyone, and for every country and every channel.

You are just 6 steps away from unstoppable international growth.

Step 1: Get Aware – take time to educate yourself and your colleagues. This way, you will all fully know the opportunities that are open to your business to grow globally using digital strategies, which will lead to a change in mindset.

Step 2: Get Ready – look at where you are now, check if your business is ready to scale internationally and get some quick wins from any existing sales and marketing digital channels.

Step 3: Get Started – set the direction you would like your business to travel in, identify your success factors and pitfalls, work out what could be feasible for you, and then get everyone on board so that they are all committed to an international digital strategy.

Step 4: Get Strategic – put together the three best scenarios for your international digital strategy, depending on how fast you would like to grow. Then check your profitability and draw up an implementation plan.

Step 5: Get Building – build your digital sales platform for each country, one at a time. Make sure you resource each project effectively and train your teams with up-to-date digital skills.

Step 6: Get Performing – launch with a bang or go with a soft launch if you prefer. Keep selling daily and reviewing performance weekly to identify how to continually improve.

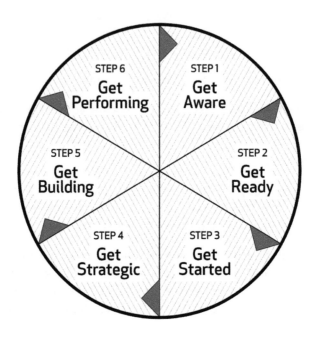

You need to become completely familiar with my method, so that it becomes like driving a car or riding a bike. You are going to go through the first 3 steps just once, as you start your preparation **(Get Aware, Get Ready and Get Started)**. Then you will need to go through the final 3 steps **(Get Strategic, Get Building and Get Performing)** for every combination of new country and new digital sales channel that you select. For example, you may get to Step 3 and realise that France could be a great place for you to sell your new innovative energy drink. At this point, you need to do more detailed research about the French market, work out the best ways to sell online to your French customers, set up a French version of your website optimised for google.fr or list your product on a French e-marketplace and then find some department stores to sell for you online and make sure they all work. So, for each new country you choose, you need to go through: **Step 4: Get Strategic, Step 5: Get Building and Step 6: Get Performing.**

Taking it to its logical conclusion, you could end up going through my method literally hundreds of times: there are five digital sales channels, 200 countries in the world and a top 10 set of world languages, so there are literally thousands of permutations for you to grow your business globally.

Copy, paste, adjust

You have to do these 6 steps in order and do not miss any out. If you do miss out any one step, you will get a sub-optimal outcome and could waste both your opportunity and investment. I mostly see companies impatiently dive straight into building a website when they become aware of the opportunity to expand international sales online. The tendency is to rush through to the end, skipping important and sometimes crucial tasks in an earlier step, only to find the cards come tumbling down. Too often, I see companies that have elevated themselves to the lofty heights of building a website in **Step 5: Get Building** after skipping the earlier steps, only to find out that they missed an important technical task in **Step 2: Get Ready**. This then throws them off course and slips them right back down to the start. It can be just like a game of snakes and ladders.

In addition, if you dive straight into devising a digital strategy in **Step 4: Get Strategic** without first spending the time and energy required in the preparatory Steps of 1 – 3, you will inevitably get caught out and may set off on the wrong track with the wrong plan. Sadly, there are a lot of businesses in this position – don't be one of them!

For long-term sustainable growth that seamlessly fits in with your business model and business development, you need to be as thorough as possible in all of these steps. You may get tempted to take a shortcut or go for an international opportunity that drops into your inbox before you are really ready. If something like this crops up while you're in the middle of doing everything according to the Grow Global Method, assess the opportunity, and if it is worth pursuing, hit pause and go for it. Then come back to the method as quickly as you can. Try not to let it derail your plans. It's a bit like when you fall off the waggon while on a healthy eating or exercise regime – if you get derailed, start again tomorrow!

My method shows you how to do everything correctly, in order, so that you can get it right first time. So take your time to carefully read through the whole of this chapter. Familiarise yourself with each of the 6 steps, so you know the task that is before you. When you've finished the book and are ready to take action, go back to the first step and work through the activity checklists. Then move on to the next step, and the next, and you'll be on your way. Get your notebook out and do this right.

You owe it to yourselves and your business to **Get Aware, Get Ready, Get Started, Get Strategic, Get Building** and then **Get Performing**, so you too can achieve unstoppable international growth.

Step 1: Get Aware

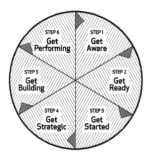

	GET AWARE
	Discover
	Opportunity
	Mindset

Step 1: Get Aware is usually a 'light bulb' moment for you, if you have not been able to see a way to grow your business either digitally or internationally before. You've overlooked how powerful using online sales can be for your business or you may have found that you have reached a plateau, as there is either saturated or sluggish demand for your product or service in your home market. Suddenly, you realise you are missing out on growth and should be taking your successful home formula to other countries.

Becoming aware of the potential sales opportunities that your business is currently ignoring can be very sobering. When you start to think of how many potential customers you are failing to reach and serve, you will become highly motivated to do something about it.

Tasks to Get Aware

Step 1: Get Aware involves the following tasks:
Discover, Opportunity and Mindset.

DISCOVER

The question you need to ask is: **What are the trends, and what is possible for my industry?**

To start this process off, you have to spend some time really understanding what are going to be the external influences that will change your industry and your business in the future, and what options are open to you. In particular, focus in on the impact that digital commerce may have in your sector, and what possibilities there are to take advantage of new technologies and digital tools within your business.

If you've already read Part A of this book, then you've already done this! If you haven't yet, go back and do that right now!

ACTIVITY: DISCOVER CHECKLIST

Take the time to browse the internet to get up to speed on the trends for the future of your industry by reading and following forward-looking organisations on Facebook or Twitter, or join webinars for an hour. The sources will, of course, be different in every country, but here are some ideas and some of my favourites for finding out about all things digital and international:

- From your industry e.g. your trade association

- National newspapers and periodicals e.g. *The Economist*

- Business organisations e.g. Chambers of Commerce

- Analyst and research organisations e.g. Gartner, Accenture

- Technology blogs and magazines e.g. *Wired, Inc*

- Future blogs and commentary e.g. World Economic Forum, Futurism.

OPPORTUNITY

The second question you need to ask yourself is: **Am I aware of the opportunity for my business?**

You might have noticed a competitor selling on eBay, or you might have spotted a new entrant taking the sector by storm with a new low-cost digital business model. Then, you see one of your biggest competitors has just won a multimillion dollar contract to build a new theatre in the UAE, as they had an Arabic section on their website. Whatever has triggered it, this is where you realise that there is a big world out there, full of potential new customers and selling through digital channels can help you to reach them. If you've not realised it was possible to sell this way, you've been missing out on a big opportunity to expand your business.

Imagine if you were able to replicate the business you are doing in your home country, in just a few new countries — say Ireland, France or Mexico — then it would really make a difference to your bottom line (even if it was just 10% of your revenue to start with)!

Once you've seen the opportunity out there, make sure everyone else in your company is aware of it as well.

ACTIVITY: OPPORTUNITY CHECKLIST

Spend an hour out of the office surfing the internet to find some inspiration that will help you to understand the opportunity that's open to your particular business:

- Are your biggest competitors already using more digital sales channels than you?

- Are there players in your sector that are more international than you?

- Are there any new entrants to your market that are taking it by storm?

- Is there a company you admire in another industry that's really doing well?

MINDSET

The third question you need to ask yourself is: **Am I in the right mindset to pull this off?**

At this point, you realise that selling online and internationally can transform your business and get your company in front of millions of new customers, so it has to be core to your future vision.

If you want to grow fast, you have to be prepared to invest. **It is not about being a cost to the business. It is an investment in the business to produce a return.** This is a completely different mindset, and it means that you will action in a completely different league.

You have to put any doubts behind you and be brave enough to make the changes that your business needs to survive and thrive in the digital age. You need to be prepared to move forward into new countries around the world, even when things are not totally certain. You'll minimise the risk by doing lots of research, so you'll know the things to look out for, but you still need to be prepared to take a leap of faith, experiment and 'give things a go', constantly evaluating what works and what doesn't for your particular business, so you can make changes quickly.

ACTIVITY: MINDSET CHECKLIST

Take an hour out of the office and go and sit somewhere quiet and relaxing and ask yourself these questions:

Are you holding any negative or defeatist thoughts?

Is there anything that is actually holding you back?

Are you feeling overwhelmed by the thought of all the change that is ahead of you?

Do you feel it might be easier to just get out of the business, as you're not cut out for this new digital age?

Are you ready to 'give it a go' and trust in the process and where it can take you?

Do you actually believe that the investment you make will pay off?

Are you excited about the prospect of what a scalable digital global business can bring?

How does Get Aware help you on your international digital journey?

It takes you from the **Educate** stage and prevents you from going into the holding pattern of the **Procrastinate** stage, as you are so keen to get ready and get started to transform your business and reap the benefits of increased international leads and sales.

What happens if you miss out the Get Aware step?

This awareness is vital to the overall success of your digital transformation and global expansion. Without this knowledge of what is possible and without this spark for chasing success, you are unlikely to give international or digital the priority or the resources they need within your business. In fact, you are very likely to be overtaken by a competitor willing to take it more seriously than you do.

**Interview with Niamh Barker,
Managing Director of The Travelwrap Company**

www.thetravelwrapcompany.com

Quite frankly, the business-to-business model was not working for us and my back was against the wall. The website was just secondary in our business and a showcase for the retailers. We were just getting dribs and drabs of orders.

In 2013, after going on a business accelerator and then talking to Sarah, I just saw the light about using the website to sell online around the world. It was the starting point of the business when I realised it was not just an expensive hobby. I made the decision to cancel all trade shows and stopped calling all the trade customers. All those exhibitions were expensive and they weren't working for us.

The profit margin wasn't big enough and the business was becoming financially unviable.

I realised the website would be vital in attracting new customers, but our old website was not helping us to reach our export potential as it was built on an outdated bespoke e-commerce platform and couldn't support other currencies. Even more of a revelation to me was that we were not appearing in search results in our target markets, such as Australia. We were essentially invisible.

I told the team we were going to focus on selling online. If you do one thing incredibly well, you are able to sell online, whereas on the high street you couldn't attract enough customers. I now get customers not only from the UK, but from overseas as well. Basically, we offer something that is the best in the world and we do it better than anyone else, creating success all over the planet.

Step 2: Get Ready

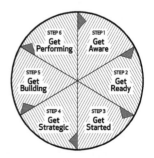

| **GET READY** |
| Baseline |
| Readiness |
| Audit |

Step 2: Get Ready involves taking a long, hard look at exactly where your business is today to make sure that you are actually ready to go international and digital. It is worth taking the time to get your house in order at home before going international. I always say you need to be world class before you can grow global.

Once you have completed this step successfully, you will have put all the building blocks in place behind the scenes and also considered the needs of your international customers. As a bonus, some early quick wins can increase online and traditional sales in your own country and improve the productivity and profitability of your whole business.

It can be a time-consuming step, depending on where your business is at the moment. For some of you, it may be the first time you've actually sat back to look at your business with an objective eye. This can be enlightening as you happily learn so much about your own company, and you will find it satisfying when you start to make immediate improvements. For others, who already have a well-structured and well-run business, this step might just involve some quick tweaks to systems and processes.

So take a deep breath, and remember the more methodical you are in preparing, the quicker and easier it will be to design and implement your plan for global digital growth. So take your time to do this properly and you'll fast track your growth.

Tasks to Get Ready

Step 2: Get Ready involves the following tasks:
Baseline, Readiness and Audit.

BASELINE

The first thing you need to ask yourself is: **Where am I now?**

Before you begin, you must take a baseline of your whole business, international and digital performance. You should have this information at your fingertips, but most companies don't. It is critical to have this data, so you can run your current business properly and track your progress as you grow globally. Going through this process is a really important step to understand how digital contributes to your international sales, if you already have some.

The good thing about digital is that you can measure the impact of almost everything you do very precisely. In contrast, if you send out a press release into the ether, it is often really hard to measure exactly what effect it has had on your business.

ACTIVITY: BASELINE CHECKLIST

Make sure that you really understand where you are getting your sales from both on and offline, country by country. Take a look at your Google Analytics, e-marketplace analytics, social media analytics and analyse how much each of your distributors or stockists are selling on your behalf in each country and whether they're doing that via digital or traditional channels. If you've not started selling internationally yet, then do this just for your home country.

You will need to document a whole series of metrics, including:

- How much are you selling into different countries?

- How much are you selling though digital and traditional channels?

- Which countries and channels are growing fastest?

- How many visitors are you getting to your digital sales platforms from around the world?

- How well are they converting into sales or leads?

- How is your website ranking globally?

- How popular are your products and services on online marketplaces?

- How well are your social media pages doing?

- Who have you sold the most to worldwide?

READINESS

The next thing you need to honestly ask yourself is: **Am I truly ready to grow globally fast?**

Being ready means that you have a world-class digital presence, and that you have back office systems, processes and teams to run an efficient and scalable business, which is as automated as possible, so that you can scale when international orders start to grow. Support your digital team with the best digital tools to increase productivity and streamline your business.

Time and again companies come to me and want to go international, but at the end of the day they end up hitting obstacles because the building blocks of their core domestic business are not in place. However, some companies investing in these tasks actually find that their business improves really quickly, and the saved time and increased productivity easily pay for the investment in new digital tools and new skills.

Digital presence not ready

When I look at a company's website, social media and wider digital presence, I often find that I really can't understand what they do or even how to get in contact with them. I don't know what is special about them and I can't see the benefits of their product or service, which is full of out-of-date information. Their digital presence is often poorly designed or substandard, and not even good enough for their home market. They are just not ready to go international. They may be getting a small number of leads online and their social media still needs some work. You have to have a sustainable, profitable business - otherwise, there is no point going fully international. Be profitable at home first.

You need to be truly world class first with a product, service and even digital presence that you are really proud of - otherwise, you will be replicating something that is sub-optimal. Remember the old '80s computing phrase 'garbage in, garbage out?' This is what happens if you try to communicate with customers from different cultures who speak other languages with something that doesn't even make sense in your own language for your home customers.

Back-end and systems not ready

Frequently, I find that companies I work with have non-existent internal business systems and processes, or if they have them, they are not automated and not fit for purpose, let alone ready to scale internationally. These companies don't have a proper accounts system or anywhere to record all of their customers, and if they sell products, they are unaware of how much stock they are holding. There are so many digital tools that can be easily implemented to make day-to-day operations much smoother and more efficient, like marketing automation, customer relationship databases, stock systems (if you're selling products) and multicurrency finance systems. But these companies are often doing things the hard way!

> *We have increasingly automated the business, so it runs itself and is scalable globally. In a nutshell, we've learnt to use technology to make our day-to-day operations very efficient.*
>
> Patrick Coghlan, CEO and Founder, Renovo International

No digital sales channels ready

Even worse, many companies I work with aren't even actually selling online and haven't even bothered to use digital strategies to actively seek out new customers. As they say, you have to be in it to win it!

I see many business-to-business customers that still rely heavily on their distributor network to reach international customers or do not make it clear to their customers that they could get a fast online quote. Even if they are not selling directly to clients and are using the third-party route of selling through distributors or stockists instead, there is no 'where to buy' information on their website. Or their product information is hard to find on a distributor or stockist website.

Service companies often don't serve their customers or deliver their services online, like an audit or a consultation that could be done through Skype or Zoom, or a client's requirements gathered via a FaceTime or WhatsApp call.

To support your digital presence and new automated internal business systems, make sure that you have a digital-savvy forward-thinking team with a digital mindset in place, as well as access to freelancers and professionals you can call on for advice and help with implementing all things international and digital.

ACTIVITY: READINESS CHECKLIST

In a perfect world, there is a lot to think about up front before you start. You will need to take a close look at all the different areas of your business to see if they are all individually ready:

Is your brand world class?

Is your content distinctive and easily understood?

Are you taking advantage of the latest digital tools?

Could you deliver any of your products or services digitally to reach more customers around the world?

Are your business systems and processes in place?

Is your team world class, forward thinking and digital savvy?

What help do you need from professionals?

You don't have all the areas in place yet? You really do need to. You are not world class, so not really ready to grow globally. You need to be ready to embrace digital in every part of your business, so you are able to scale internationally as your business grows. If an international opportunity does come in while you're in the **Get Ready** step, you will need to assess if you can take it on without disrupting your business in your home country and consider if you can serve it fully. Whatever decision you make, be sure to keep moving forward with the process of putting all these building blocks in place.

AUDIT

If you are ready, then ask yourself: **Can I get some quick wins?**

If you've already got a website or online marketplace listing, take the time to audit each of your existing digital sales channels. Firstly, identify quick wins that will start to make a difference from day one. You will find opportunities to make your international digital sales platforms look so much better and clearer, and also achieve some increased sales, both in your home country and internationally. You may even pay for all your investment in this task by quickly increasing online leads and sales.

You need to check that what you are doing now is best practice. As it will be the foundation and launch pad for everything you do going forward, make sure that you are operating at a level that is as world class as possible.

Do an audit of all your digital sales channels: your website, your e-marketplace listings and any social selling you have set up. If you have partners, like distributors or stockists, work with them to see how they can improve their digital presence. Focus on compiling a list of actions that you can quickly implement over the next three months.

ACTIVITY: AUDIT CHECKLIST

Take a critical look at your own digital sales channels to see if they are appealing to international customers:

- Is your brand and logo suitable for international visitors?

- Will customers in other countries understand what you do?

- Are your images, videos and content relevant for international customers?

- Does your company story clearly tell people from other countries in plain and simple language why you are so great and so different?

- Have you checked that people in other countries use the same terminology as people in your own country?

- Have you made sure that everything is optimised for the best possible visibility in search engines around the world?

- Are you sure everything is optimised for mobile speeds in different countries and online visibility worldwide?

- Are you sure you are compliant with all legal terms and conditions for the country you are selling into?

How does Get Ready help you on your international digital journey?

By being methodical and getting all your back office systems and processes in place and improving your existing digital presence for international visitors, you can move on up to the **Orientate** stage of the international digital journey, without even touching the **Deviate** stage. However, don't get stuck in the **Procrastinate** stage by waiting until everything is completely perfect. Instead, do enough to be able to move forward with purpose with the building blocks in place, formalising everything as you grow (as they say 'imperfect action is better than perfect inaction').

What happens if you miss out the Get Ready step?

Solid preparation is vital. If you miss out on this step or rush through it without giving it proper attention, you will find that you keep hitting obstacles that slow you down or eventually cause you just to give up. You'll also find that without the quick wins early on, it can become demoralising and you'll miss out on both productivity savings and increased sales.

Interview with Robert Lancaster, Managing Director of Trinca-Ferro

www.trinca-ferro.com

It looks so much different from the early days. We had to switch from our original e-commerce platform early on to allow us more flexibility in adding the different local online stores and removed the Google Translate facility in favour of using a professional translator. Google Translate is OK for some things, but not ideal to promote a company's messages in another language in an accurate way, such as producing high quality content, rich product descriptions and blogs in German and Brazilian Portuguese. It is critical for a new brand to be communicated correctly in the local language.

We've overhauled absolutely everything, including adding new and better product images. We've spent a lot of time continually improving our website, adding all sorts of content, like blogs and press coverage, as well as working on search engine optimisation. This has really paid off, as we're much more visible in search engines. Even technical aspects have been improved, like increasing the site speed to get a good response time in all the countries we're targeting and adopting the trend to make the website secure.

We are now looking to consolidate the growth in the countries we are already in and also to spend time going back and systemising the business and finding ways to increase the profitability, which we didn't really do at the beginning. Then we're poised to look for new countries and new channels!

Step 3: Get Started

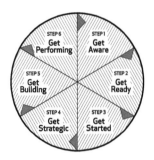

GET STARTED

Direction
Feasibility
Commit

Step 3: Get Started is an exciting step, and one where you will really **begin** to see what is possible as you take concrete steps towards completely transforming your business.

At this point, you understand that you need to move fast in this new international and digital age, which is already upon you, so that you don't miss out and get left behind. You are motivated to get started.

Tasks to Get Started

Step 3: Get Started involves the following tasks:
Direction, Feasibility and Commit.

DIRECTION

Now you need to ask yourself this question: **Where do I want to be in three years?**

You have determined where you are now in your baseline activity, but now I want you to think about what your business would like to achieve in international sales over the next three years. You are transforming your business from 'A' to 'B', so you need to map out exactly what B will look like for your particular business. It will be different for everyone, but having an end point in sight will keep you focused on your goal. This is the point at which you can dream a bit!

If you've already done some work on business planning, then make sure you can now see where digital fits in. If you don't have a business plan yet, then start to put one together. I'm not talking about pages and pages of detailed plans. You could use a digital tool like LivePlan which takes you through it step-by-step and can even monitor your progress against your plan automatically by integrating with your finance system. It would be truly awesome to have sub-plans, such as an international or export plan, a marketing plan, a sales plan, a social media plan and content plan to name but a few, but I don't want you to get paralysed into inaction here. So use another digital tool like Trello to keep a list of your key activities (which are then very easy to move around if your business changes direction a bit, which it will). Setting the future direction for your new business is a fluid activity that needs to be revisited every quarter if you're in a fast-moving sector.

ACTIVITY: DIRECTION CHECKLIST

You need to work out what international growth you want for your business. Ask yourself the following:

- What are your overall business objectives?

- What level of international sales do you want to achieve?

- What would success really look like for you?

- How fast do you want to grow?

- Do you have the capacity?

- Do you have the budget?

FEASIBILITY

The question you must answer now is this: **Is there going to be enough demand for my products and services in other countries to make this viable?**

It is crucial to determine if there is demand for your products and services internationally and are there actually customers who are searching for or buying your products and services online in other countries around the world. You don't need to do a full market research exercise at this point. Take more of a rough and ready look at what is possible for your own business and work out if there are any big opportunities or showstopping obstacles for your business internationally.

Depending on your sector, there are many things that you need to look at that will influence whether a country is suitable, such as regulations (e.g. for foods or medicines), the level of compliance (e.g. fire regulations for clothing or furniture), accreditations or qualification recognition (e.g. for a lawyer or accountant) and customs duties (which can be up to 80% in some countries for some product categories). There are other factors that may influence your choice of country too, like having personal connections in a country, making use of languages that your team already speak, as well as how easy it is to do business and how far away the country is geographically.

Take your top five bestselling products and services and do some initial online research, using the checklist below.

There's a lot you can do. Look particularly for your competitors online and note which digital sales channels they are using to both generate leads and make sales in different countries. Of course, you will need to speak the language to do this research yourself in another country that doesn't speak your language.

Just a note about your competitors – they might not be the ones you expected them to be, as different countries operate different business models. For example, you may sell homeware and find that your biggest competitor in a certain country is actually a fashion brand. They may be famous for couture not curtains, but they could have leveraged that brand to develop a successful homeware line, so be prepared for surprises. Also, don't just follow the pack. Just because a competitor has gone to Australia, doesn't mean it is right for you. Do your own research.

ACTIVITY: RESEARCH CHECKLIST

You need to start off with some exploratory research, to see if your bestselling products or services are likely to be in demand in another country:

- Is your actual product or service already being sold in that country successfully (e.g. through distributors, stockists, retailers or online)?

- Who are your top competitors?

- Are your competitors selling similar products and services?

- How popular are your products and services in other countries?

- Is your product or service relevant to customers in other countries?

- Does your product or service need adapting for a new market?

- Are there any research reports on your sector in that country?

- Are there any regulatory or certification requirements in your sector?

- Are there any barriers to entry or restrictions that are going to put your costs up?

- Are similar products or services appearing on websites in the local version of Google e.g. google.com.au for Australia. Are these being sold by competitors or by a company that could become your distributor or stockist?

- Are similar products and services appearing on local online marketplaces e.g. local Amazon or say Trade Me in New Zealand

- Does your product or service appear when you search on global or local social media sites e.g. Facebook or VK

- Is anyone selling through social media stores?

- What's the rough selling price?

- Are there any gaps in the market that your product or service could fill?

All of this research will feed into your international digital strategy. You will do your full market research in the next step: **Get Strategic.**

COMMIT

The question you must answer now is: **Am I ready to commit to selling through digital channels and internationally?**

Now you should be able to make a go/no go decision about whether you will start committing larger amounts of time and budget to take your business digital and global.

Alongside your objectives, you need to be absolutely signed up for your obligations in this process. Your success will depend on your willingness to:

- Embrace a high degree of the transformation in your business
- Sign up to change business models
- Redesign business processes
- Invest in systems, tools and training with hard cash.

You have to be ready, world class and committed to investment. Without this, you will either fail outright, deviate in another direction or fail to achieve the optimal result.

Even if it looks like your international digital project 'has legs', you must only move forward to the next step: **Get Strategic** if you are truly committed. Such commitment is vital as this is the point at which it becomes a sustained transformation programme that will replicate your business across the world, country by country, digital channel by digital channel. This can last for many years if you choose to enter multiple new international markets with different digital sales channels, but the business growth you'll see will be phenomenal. Digital and international may start as small branches of your business, but they will grow to become solid and integral parts. It is not a walk in the park. But remember, help is at hand!

ACTIVITY: COMMITMENT CHECKLIST

You need to be honest and ask yourself some tough questions before moving forward:

- Is everyone absolutely committed to digital?

- Are you really up for it?

- Do you have what it takes?

- Is everyone in the business truly committed to going international?

- What is the one big thing you need to do in the business that will allow you to commit?

- How much extra time do you really have to devote to this?

- Where is this international digital project on your list of priorities?

- How much money do you have to invest in this now, and then three years forward?

- What would you invest to get a million dollars back?

- Are you really signed up for the fact the business could look very different at the end? It may even be unrecognisable?

- Do you really believe this can transform your business right now?

How does Get Started help you on your international digital journey?

By doing the **Get Started** step, you can avoid the **Deviate** stage of the international digital journey completely, as you'll be setting your business up for success from the start. You will also stop yourself from rushing off to the **Get Strategic** step and jumping into investing in something that is fundamentally not really feasible.

Just as importantly, you will have everyone in the business on board, getting agreement on where you want to go, so that you can go full steam ahead through **Dedicate, Duplicate, Replicate,** right up to **Proliferate.**

What happens if you miss out the Get Started step?

I find that businesses who don't set a direction and think through it properly, head off haphazardly and lose their way, as they didn't work out if there was any demand there in the first place. If they're not really committed, then they tend to give up after three to six months, without giving it a chance.

**Interview with Sarah Carroll,
Founder of Grow Global**

www.growglobal.com

I decided that I wanted to take a dose of my own medicine and make Grow Global into an international and digital business.

I sat down and did a lot of analysis, looking back at which of our services had sold the best and which would be suitable for international clients. Our workshops were one of our most popular services, but our reach was limited as we were

---

running them face-to-face with 15 companies attending at a time in just the UK. I knew I could 'digitise' this offering by building these workshops as online courses, so that they would be immediately available to anyone, anywhere in the world.

We then wanted to see which countries were open to online learning and where we might be able to sell well in the future. I carried out a market selection service, which was really enlightening. I was asked to think about all the factors that would be driving demand for our online services, as well as some of the barriers. In a discussion with my market research expert, we came up with a few important factors: the ability to speak English (my courses were in English, so this was a sensible starting point to do this before translating them into other languages); credit rating (the ability to get paid, as I ask for upfront payment online); sophistication of the internet (customers would need a pretty good internet connection to access slideshows and videos online); the number of people employed in a country (my services were aimed at people in work); the size of the e-learning market (to see where customers might be more familiar with online courses). He popped this all into a very clever market selection tool he has.

What I loved about this process is it threw up some amazing reports on the size of the e-learning market globally, which have been invaluable to my understanding of the worldwide market for online courses. But it was also backed by hard statistics, not just a whim or gut feeling. The output from this market selection exercise was a grid showing me which countries to tackle first, from Australia, which is a smaller market but easier to enter, right through to Nigeria, which would be a harder market to tackle, but has enormous potential in terms of its love of education and working population size. The idea is that I start with the smaller, easier markets first to trial my services and approach, then move around the grid to bigger markets. Obviously, I need to research each of the countries in more depth in the next stage, but at least I have a list of my priorities to start from.

Step 4: Get Strategic

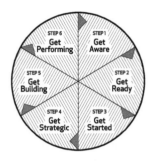

GET STRATEGIC
Proposal
Profitability
Plan

By now you know there is demand for your products and services, so you need to pick the right country to sell into and then you have to pick the right digital channel. Only move to **Step 4: Get Strategic** if you are ready and committed – if not, go back and improve the rest of your business so that it is world class and ready to scale internationally first.

This step brings together the work that you have done in **Get Ready** and **Get Started**, where you selected the best options for your business with its particular circumstances and then put together a practical, workable plan to grow globally through digital sales channels. This is when the plan for the future of your business becomes real and very exciting, but it is also when the hard work begins. Step 4 is a chunky step that many businesses want to ignore, and jump instead straight into building an international website or listing on an international e-marketplace. By now, you know the importance of doing things methodically, so get ready to roll your sleeves up.

Tasks to Get Strategic

Step 4: Get Strategic involves the following tasks:
Proposal, Profitability and Plan.

PROPOSAL

The main question that you want to ask yourself is: **How fast do I want to grow globally?**

There are alternative routes for you to get to your business objectives that depend on how fast you would like to grow globally. You need to select the best strategy for your company's ambitions, as well as your products and services and the resources you have available right now. You need to develop a range of proposals and fully cost out each option to make sure they are going to bring you the return that you need. I'm going to call our three proposals, *Play It Safe*, *Grow At Pace* and *Win The Race*. This is a crucial step to take where all the design and thinking takes place. You will need to fully map out each one so that you can make an informed decision about what is best for your business. I'll run you through the philosophy of safe, pace and race below.

Safe

For the *Safe Strategy*, you might just decide to test your first new country with a low-key market entry strategy, say listing 10 of your products on one local version of Amazon, eBay or another online marketplace if you're selling products, or putting up a 10-page local website for clients in another country if you're offering services. You won't need to invest too much time or money, and it is likely to take you between one and three months to implement. The fact that you haven't invested much, means you are probably going to get a smaller return. Nonetheless, it is a good start and does take you to the **Duplicate** stage on your international digital journey. You'll be playing it safe.

Pace

For a *Pace Strategy*, you might plan to develop an e-commerce website that features 20 or more of your most popular products and caters for three different currencies. You could target the USA first, then Canada, followed by Australia. As a service company, you'll expand your 10-page website to two other countries and add lots of localised content, like a blog or case study section featuring international projects or testimonials and news from those countries. You will also need to get language speakers on board to work with clients in those countries. This will require a decent investment in terms of both time and money, and it is likely to take you between three and six months to complete. It will put you well and truly on the digital world map and take you to the Replicate stage on your international digital journey. You can grow at pace.

Race

For a *Race Strategy*, you might plan to go all out and tackle multiple digital channels in multiple countries, developing your own multicurrency and multilingual e-commerce website on a flexible platform like Magento, and listing on many different online marketplaces across the world, including some local or niche ones in different countries. For selling services, you could start to set up separate parts of your website with content targeted to, say, 10 different countries, supported by professionals who speak the languages of those new markets. It will require a sustained investment in terms of both time and money, and does not have a timescale – this is just how you run your company now. You could even be rolling out to a new country every three months. You're going to take new markets by storm and this will take you to the **Proliferate** stage on your international digital journey. You're putting everything in to win the race. This is when unstoppable international growth kicks in.

As your three proposals emerge and start to take shape, keep researching every little detail, so that you get familiar with how your international digital sales platforms will look and play out. You can start to visualise it – a bit like a sportsperson when they are preparing for race day.

Now you understand the different aims of each proposal, it's time to get down to work. Each proposal (safe, pace and race) needs to include full market research into the selection of:

- Markets to enter
- Languages to use
- Customers to target
- Products and services to sell
- Digital sales channels to use.

Markets to enter

Prioritise the order you research the markets, based on your results of the most promising markets that you carried out in the Feasibility task.

It is important to do a lot of research to determine what your best export markets are. You will need to consider countries with the highest GDP per capita or GDP growth, or you might want to consider other factors, such as the ease of doing business or ease of trading across borders, as well as the demand for products and services in your sector and how crowded it is.

Traditionally, the internet has been a US thing, but that has all changed. There are many other markets out there that you need to research and put on your shortlist.

Companies traditionally tend to start doing business with countries that have a close geographical proximity. So, for example, if you are in Australia, you might do business in New Zealand first, or if you are a UK business, it might be Ireland first, then Belgium, France and Germany. If you've got seasonal products or services e.g. sunglasses or ski holidays, you might find that a country in the opposite hemisphere to you is just perfect. Picking other countries in your region where your nation has a trade agreement can also be a sensible starting place, like the North America Free Trade Area (NAFTA) or the European Union (EU), as it cuts down on some of the administrative complexity of trading across borders, as well as customs duties.

However, as you know, the digital world is changing and you might want to think about other economies as well. Once you are more experienced at selling internationally online, you can get an early mover advantage in new countries. While the largest number of online users live in China and India, these may not be the easiest markets to do business with initially as they are geographically vast and there are still restrictions on setting up foreign businesses there. Singapore has been ranked as the country where it is easiest to do business in the world, so you could start doing business there and then reach out to other parts of Asia, where over half of all potential global online customers are. Indonesia and Malaysia are in the top 10 countries with the largest number of internet users, but you need to find out if people in these countries are likely to have the money and desire to buy your particular goods or services. Do not forget, however, that it might be worth investing now in order to get an early mover advantage. By following my method and planning it out, adding new countries bit by bit, you can start to sell to customers online in those countries too.

Languages to use

The best approach to selecting the languages you want to do business in is to go for the low hanging fruit, so start off with customers that speak the same language as you.

English speakers, depending on their products or services, could perhaps do business with the USA, Australia, New Zealand, Canada, South Africa, the UK and Ireland. They could maybe choose India too, as well as many countries in Africa (certainly Nigeria has one of the biggest English speaking online populations), the Caribbean, Singapore and Hong Kong. There are 1.75 billion people with a working knowledge of English[15], so trading online only in English has huge potential. That may well be more than enough customers to last you a lifetime! If Spanish or French are your first languages, there are 21 countries where Spanish is an official language and about 50 countries (including some beautiful islands) where French is spoken. Again, this will give you tremendous opportunity to trade in other countries with relative ease.

Next, see if you already have any language speakers in your business with the skills to help you develop your business in a new country, and then think about employing new team members with language skills, or have a freelance linguist on call for when you need support in a particular language.

Customers to target

You will need to identify who your customers will be. While the type of customer you sell to at home is a great starting point, don't assume your customer in another country will be exactly the same. For example, they may be from a different age group, or be a smaller, lower revenue company than you are used to in your home country. People in different countries have different cultures and preferences, and there is a whole academic discipline of cross-cultural awareness, which you can read more about if it interests you. The main point is to be open-minded and realise that your customers in another country may be quite different to your home customers.

Products and services to sell

You need to work out which products and services you will sell internationally. Generally, the 80/20 rule applies to most businesses, in that you receive 80% of your revenue from 20% of your products and services. You already know which of your products and services already sell well (from **Step 2: Get Ready**), now explore whether your bestselling products and services will sell well in your target country and if they are relevant to customers there, or if the product or service needs adapting e.g. changing clothes sizes or plugs for electrical products, or changing the delivery method for services, such as using Skype or an online course. Companies who offer niche products and services tend to do better internationally, as it is something that is desirable or not easy to get access to in another country.

Digital sales channels to use

Will you be selling direct to consumers online? Will you sell through the online platform of a third-party partner like a large department store, a small retailer or wholesale distributors? For each country, you need to carefully choose the appropriate digital sales channel to sell online for each country (it might differ from country to country). It is critical that you select the right ones for your business and your sector. It is very likely that your approach will be different, say, in Europe, where you might sell through your website, compared to China, where you will sell through e-marketplaces and s-commerce, and Latin America, where you sell through online stockists or distributors, for example.

As a reminder, here are your five main digital sales channels for reaching international customers:

- International website (lead generation)
- International e-commerce website
- International e-marketplaces
- International s-commerce
- Selling through partners online.

There are particular things to consider when choosing your digital sales channels, such as establishing if there are any logistical and financial considerations at this point, if you're selling products through e-commerce, including potential shipping costs, delivery times and local rates of customs duties.

If you're selling through e-marketplaces, the big players may not be for everyone. Where you should list really does depend on your business sector, products and services. A specialist marketplace might be more appropriate, depending on your product. For example, if you sell fashion accessories and jewellery, it could be worth starting with the global fashion marketplaces before investigating a local fashion marketplace. Once you've selected one or two, you can quite easily test your product or service in new countries by selling on e-marketplaces in a 'safe' environment.

It is also a wise digital strategy to spread the load across multiple online marketplaces, as I know of clients who have had their products dropped or stores closed at short notice on some of the biggest online marketplaces, although this is a rare occurrence, I am relieved to say.

For service companies, it is important to check if there are any restrictions that could affect the delivery of your services. For example, if you need any specialised qualifications in a particular country or if there will be visa requirements when you visit in person.

So which proposal should you go for?

By now you should have three detailed proposals: *Play It Safe*, *Grow At Pace* and *Win The Race*, and each of these should include: markets to enter, languages to use, customers to target, products and services to sell and digital sales channels to use.

I know it can feel a bit overwhelming at this stage, so my advice to help you decide which proposal to go for is similar to what your parents sagely told you about buying a property – go for as much as you can, but don't overstretch yourself. Results come from where you put your focus, and you don't want to bite off more than you can chew, however exciting the 'race' might seem.

Look at which proposal feels doable in the next year. You can always change gear and move up from 'play it safe' to 'grow at pace'. Or you can even – if you find you've been too ambitious and your growth is too fast – move down from 'win the race' to 'grow at pace'.

A last word of advice – whichever proposal you choose, it is always best to enter one country at a time and build up one channel at a time. Only move on to the next one once the initial country or channel is fully optimised and performing. Again, **copy, paste, adjust**.

ACTIVITY: MARKET RESEARCH CHECKLIST

You now need to build on the research that you did in the 'Feasibility' task, to do more market research. It is important to continually do thorough research to learn as much as possible about your new country, looking at some of these statistics and sources, including:

- GDP per capita/GDP growth

- PPP per capita/PPP growth

- Distance from home

- Languages spoken

- Number of internet users

- Number of mobile internet users

- Size of e-commerce market

- Size of the m-commerce market

- Sector size e.g. sector, legal

- How easy it is to do business and get paid e.g. Ease of Doing Business Index

- How peaceful a country is e.g. Global Peace Index

- Corruption in the country e.g. Corruption Perception Index

- How much is sold online in that country through each digital channel?

- Who would be your perfect customer in your new country?

- Are you going to sell direct to consumers or via other businesses?

- What are the costs of delivery, custom duties, sales tax, legal documentation etc.?

- Can you deliver digital products or services instead?

- Which domain names are available and in use?

- Which social media names are available and in use?

Remember that libraries, trade associations, chambers of commerce, local embassies or the inward investment arm of a trade promotion agency often hold research reports, which can be downloaded from their websites, which can be tremendously helpful in setting the scene for your sector or the digital landscape in a new country.

PROFITABILITY

The next question you need to ask yourself is: **Do I have a big enough margin to do this?**

Do take your time to cost each proposal (Safe, Pace and Race) to see which will be most profitable for you and where the breakeven point actually is. Remember that the cost includes the opportunity cost of not doing other things in your business. There is also the time it takes you and your team, not just the costs you might pay to register a website domain name or pay a website developer.

You need to make sure that each product range or service is profitable to sell in each country. **There is no point preparing a strategy or starting to build your digital sales platforms, if it is not going to be profitable for you.** We have had clients selling their products on amazon.de who realised after three months they were not actually making any money at all. In fact, they were losing a significant amount per sale when everything was factored in. I want to save you that pain up front.

Take the cost of manufacturing or buying in your product, or designing and delivering your service, then start to look at the true costs. Some of the more common ones are listed below, but there will be specific costs for your business if you are in e-commerce or shipping large products across the world in containers. Get a spreadsheet up and list absolutely everything you can think of. It's better to be safe than sorry. This is pure maths.

ACTIVITY: MARGIN CHECKLIST

You need to analyse all the core costs of your international digital sales platform, both the overheads and variable costs, including:

- Domain names

- Website hosting

- Website platform

- Web design

- Web development

- Photographs and images

- Video production

- Copywriting

- Translation

- Digital marketing

- Digital marketing executive

- Multilingual customer support

- Payment method fee

- Currency conversion fee.

PLAN

The question you want to answer now is: **How can I get the best results?**

To implement most international digital strategies these days, businesses need a comprehensive plan and the best skills and know-how to actually make it happen. You don't want to take on too much and you need to make sure that you achieve the results in each task well.

You need to prepare a full plan for your chosen international digital strategy. I am a big believer in breaking everything down into much smaller, more manageable projects and tasks. I would view each country and each channel as a separate project and prepare a mini business plan for each. The project plan is a living document that will change as the project evolves. You will get more experienced in implementing new digital sales channels, as you learn more and more about your new countries and how best to do business there. So each time you'll get better results, faster.

Given that you are likely to implement this approach time and time again, it is worth taking the time to set up your project plan on a digital tool, like Trello, Todoist, Asana or Basecamp or even Microsoft Project, so you can then reuse it for each new country and each new digital sales channel.

As this task is so critical to your business, it's important to find the right person to take responsibility for it, even if you have to get someone in from outside your business with the experience to make it happen and get it right first time.

If you're planning a complex e-commerce build, then it would be advisable to complete a website specification document, especially when building an international one, as many website developers are unfamiliar with how best to do this. This specification will detail exactly what needs to be in an international website, including the navigation tabs, the country and language targeting, and the payment methods to be integrated.

ACTIVITY: PLAN CHECKLIST

You need to produce a project plan that includes:

- Goals and objectives
- Timescales
- Milestones
- Tasks
- Resources
- Budgets
- Risks
- Issues
- Track costs
- Change control
- Sign-off.

How does Get Strategic help you on your international digital journey?

This step makes sure that you choose the right country to **Duplicate** into and gives you a process to follow each time you **Replicate** your business in a new country or new digital sales channel.

What happens if you miss out the Get Strategic step?

I find that people who do this end up literally hopping all over the world, half-heartedly trying new markets without any co-ordination or prioritisation, based on a whim rather than any proper research into whether there is demand for their products and services there. While they might achieve some positive results, these are likely to be sub-optimal and they could even lose money. In addition, they will not be building up a process they can apply again and again for new markets and new digital sales channels. I see many companies that don't pick the right market, don't pick the right channel and don't plan.

**Interview with Robert Lancaster,
Managing Director of Trinca-Ferro**

www.trinca-ferro.com

Once the website was selling well in the UK, I decided to explore new markets and other digital channels to create more revenue. We did lots of analysis when expanding and this data helped me to decide which were the best digital channels and which were the best countries to prioritise.

In the UK, the website was complemented with listings on Amazon, as well as eBay. We also listed on Etsy and Notonthehighstreet, which were both very successful and sales have been building month on month.

I first dipped into new international markets with Etsy, as well as Amazon in the USA, with very positive results, which showed me there was potential in other countries. In fact, I concluded it was better to invest in Etsy in the USA in the first place, rather than investing in the website, to test the market first on what is an established marketplace.

Then we went back to the website and started with an English-speaking market and created the Australian website, adding it to our main website. Within a month of launching the new Australian site, we were enjoying regular and growing sales, so then moved on to the USA site.

With the success in the English-speaking markets, I decided to move to foreign language territories – Brazil where I was really familiar with the market, and Germany where I researched and knew the products would do well. We've now developed my multilingual website and added German and Brazilian pages.

I took the time to work out how much it would cost to purchase my knobs in India, as well as how much it would cost to deliver to every single market.

Step 5: Get Building

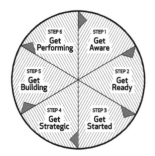

| **GET BUILDING**
Resource
Build
Train

Step 5: Get Building is the step you've been itching to get to. This can be both the most exhilarating and exasperating step in my whole method. One thing is for sure – it is the point at which all your work and planning starts paying off and begins to come to life.

Once you've got the green light from all the previous steps and your plans are in place to 'Play It Safe', 'Grow At Pace' or 'Win The Race', then it is finally time to come into **Step 5: Get Building.**

You need to follow your chosen strategy and plan from the **Get Strategic** phase, starting with one country and one digital sales channel first. Work hard to make sure that the initial one is performing first, before starting the next one. The key element here is to make sure you have everything in place to implement your strategy and plan impeccably.

Tasks to Get Building

Step 5: Get Building involves the following tasks:
Resource, Build and Train.

RESOURCE

The main question you need to answer is: **Have I got the right team around me to implement this quickly?**

One of the reasons any companies do not achieve their full potential in selling internationally and online is that they do not put the right team in place. I often see companies taking on an marketing graduate or intern with no experience of digital or the international arenas they are put in charge of. Through no fault of their own, they are unable to see strategically, as they are not familiar enough with the business and tactically don't even know where to start as they don't have the specialist skills. You can imagine how this pans out, so make sure your company does not make this mistake.

Instead, you need a whole host of specialist digital and international skills to help you implement your plan. You can get hold of these in three ways:

- Do it yourself in-house by recruiting people with the right skills
- Train up your existing team members with digital skills
- Hire external agency experts in that already have the experience and keep themselves on the cutting edge.

I often see that in-house teams can only get you so far, then you need to get in more specialist skills to truly achieve the growth in digital sales that you deserve. It will always be a trade-off between costs and how fast you would like to grow globally.

Often, the best approach is to have an in-house project manager who is employed by you. Then you can build up a virtual team around you of the right digital specialists you need at the right time to make sure the implementation happens on time and is impeccable. They will all be managed by your project manager, who will manage multiple digital projects at one go, as set out in the plan. You are looking for a new type of person to join your team that may look very different from your existing team members, who could have been with your company for many years and excelled at traditional sales and marketing. You may have some difficult decisions to make about your team as your business model transforms to a digital and international one.

Your project manager will need to make sure all the pieces of the jigsaw fit together to get the best possible result. This can be tricky. You will need regular progress reports (at least every two weeks) based upon all your digital sales and digital marketing analytics. In addition, you will need regular strategy and planning sessions (monthly or at least quarterly, depending on how fast you want to grow).

Doing it in-house

This can be a good starting point. If you don't have the necessary skills in your team, you can recruit team members, but you may not be able to find all the skills you need in one person. You also need to make sure that you retain the core team members if your international digital strategy depends on them, or at least have a succession plan in place if they leave your business. Hire the best team members you can. Make sure that some of your team have experience of working in the international arena, such as someone of a different nationality who has language skills, understands the business culture and can help with customer sales and support.

In your in-house team, you need to have:

- Committed leaders, whether they be the founders, directors or board members
- A digital champion and an international champion, fighting the corner for your project to make sure it gets the priority and resources it needs to succeed
- An international digital strategy manager, who acts as your project manager.

This team should be small and nimble. A single team member could adopt more than one of these roles in a smaller business. This is a full-time job, so it is not to be shared with a traditional marketing role and will be much wider than just an e-commerce manager.

Hiring experts

Employing digital agencies or freelancers is a great way of getting up-to-date digital skills immediately, but you have to make sure that they really understand your strategy and your plan, and that you have a positive working relationship. They are not employed by you, so are unlikely to have as much vested interest and passion in the project as you and your team, as they may work for many different clients at the same time. So make sure your project is getting the attention it deserves. Always get quotes from three different suppliers and ask for three references from previous customers. Hire the best supplier you can possibly afford. You may also want to hire a translator or employ a local digital marketing agency in another country. They will bring language skills and insight into the local culture and business practices, before you need someone full-time who is dedicated to a particular country.

These days the level of digital skills needed in each specialist area are very deep. For example, it's unlikely that an SEO expert will be an expert on LinkedIn or a Magento developer an expert in Instagram. It is unlikely that you will find all of these skills in any one marketing or web development person, so be open to getting skills from different sources.

ACTIVITY: DIGITAL SKILLS CHECKLIST

You need to make sure you have the core digital and international skills that your project requires, including:

- Content production (copy, images, video, blogs)

- Website design and development

- E-commerce management

- E-marketplace set up

- Social media shop set up

- Social media posting

- Online advertising (PPC across different digital marketing channels from Google AdWords to Facebook Ads to Amazon)

- Project management

- Working with partners in other countries

- Digital tools (analytics, e-newsletters etc.)

- Translation

- Language skills.

BUILD

The question that you need to know the answer to is: **Do I have all the component parts I need to launch my new digital sales channel?**

During this task, you will build out your chosen digital sales channel, whether it be a website, e-commerce website, e-marketplace, s-commerce, or working with your partners to boost their online presence in their local country.

You will have to implement it really well, whether it is your in-house team or your digital agency who is doing the work. Make sure that everything is built to best practice and is truly world class and set up with international visitors in mind.

I find that actually the 'technical' build, like building the e-commerce website or setting up an e-marketplace listing, is the 'easy' part if you're using a specialist. Many projects actually get delayed as the 'content' or 'assets' to go onto the digital sales platform are not available and take a long time to develop and get up to the required standard, such as the images, the product or service descriptions. This is why you need to do the Readiness task in **Step 2: Get Ready upfront.**

It can be really fast building 10 product listings on Amazon or setting up a Facebook Shop and you can have everything done, so that it is ready to be in front of customers across the globe in just a single day. On the other hand, a full large-scale e-commerce website is likely to take between three and six months to design, build, test and launch. You will need to get all your content and digital assets ready alongside your digital sales platform build.

ACTIVITY: CONTENT CREATION CHECKLIST

You need to have this basic list of content ready to slot into your new digital sales platform, including:

- Logo
- Strapline
- 100-word overview about your company
- Your unique selling point (USPs)
- Product and service descriptions
- Product images
- Banner images
- 'About Us' page
- Company video
- Testimonials
- Cases studies
- Accreditations and awards
- Legals (including, terms and conditions, privacy policy, cookie policy)
- Social media pages
- Translations.

The great thing about preparing all the content together is that it can be used over and over again in every digital sales channel and in every country, so it is the great base you need to localise everything as you go along (images, language, culture).

ACTIVITY: BUILD CHECKLIST

Once you're ready to go, get all your technical building blocks in place by:

- Reserving all your digital 'real estate', such as website domain names for each country

- Creating accounts or business pages with all the relevant social media networks to reserve your name, even if you are not going to use them at the moment

- Selecting a high-performance website hosting company

- Starting your website or e-commerce build

- Applying for your online marketplace accounts

- Setting up all your payment methods e.g. PayPal, Stripe.

TRAIN

The main question to answer here is: **Can my team get the best out of our new digital sales platform, so that it performs as optimally as possible?**

With so much new digital technology and new business processes in place, you must absolutely train your teams up in any new skills they might need, from technical updates to a Magento website to using Google Search Console.

ACTIVITY: TRAINING CHECKLIST

Continually upskill your teams over a period of time to make sure they can efficiently run and optimise your new digital sales platform and the processes surrounding them, including:

- Adding product or service information to a WordPress or Magento website platform

- Handling leads or sales, according to a best practice process

- Setting up project management software

- Reading analytics software e.g. Google Analytics or Amazon Insights

- Managing Google Search Console or Bing Webmaster Tools

- Optimising the digital sales platform e.g. tweaking SEO on a website or refining search terms in Amazon

- Reporting performance at regular intervals.

How does Get Building help you on your international digital journey?

When you have implemented this step 'Get Building' successfully, you will move up the international digital journey from 'Orientate' to 'Dedicate' and beyond. You will have put in place a solid digital sales platform that you can continue to work on, so that is starts to bring you the leads and sales you need. By doing things properly, it will stop you from slipping back into the 'Deviate' or 'Procrastinate' stages, so you won't get disillusioned and lose momentum.

What happens if you miss out the Get Building step?

I find that people often rush through the build phase and don't implement a truly world-class digital sales platform. They often take shortcuts or do it on the cheap, like not investing in great images or copy and missing out the SEO during the build or getting an intern to build the site. If they're setting up online marketplace listings, they don't take the time to put the right search terms into the back end. Later on, they then can't see why they are not getting the results for increasing their leads or sales. Or even if they have built something, they miss out on the training, so don't have the skills to run it, maintain it and manage it successfully, so once again don't get optimal results. Digital implementation projects typically take so much longer than they need to do. Every day that your new digital sales channel is not launched, is another day of lost leads and sales.

**Interview with Barney Dines,
CEO, Heritage Parts Centre**

www.heritagepartscentre.com

We've focused on building a digital savvy team around us. We have digital marketing specialists and content strategists in our team, as well as a technology manager who oversees the integration of all our various digital platforms. We work with a range of digital agencies that work with Magento, SEO and paid search, like Google AdWords.

We realised early on that it was crucial to have language skills in our business if we wanted to go international. We have team members who speak about 10 languages, including German, Spanish, Italian, French, Flemish, Portuguese and Polish, and we're starting to work with a colleague in Indonesia now. Our language speakers work in our business-to-business sales team, in the telesales teams, helping customers over the phone and in our digital marketing teams, looking after social media. More than this, they also have local knowledge about how people tick in that country and often have contacts there to get us started.

We've spent a lot of time getting the product descriptions right on the website and adding more and more content to give our website visitors as much information as possible. We've worked this year to extend our descriptions to be 500 characters long. This helps us to share online the in-depth knowledge of our sales team here, so our customers make the right purchase in the first place. It also reduces the number of enquiries we get by phone and email, so reducing our cost of sale, while helping us with our SEO. Our returns are down under 5%, which we're really happy about.

We also spend a lot of time with our heads down in analytics tools, like Google Analytics and Moz, really understanding what is going on and finding ways to improve every aspect of what we do online.

One thing that we've found really important in increasing conversion, is to add new payment methods. We started with PayPal and credit cards, but we saw that customers in Germany, in particular, were abandoning the website at the checkout process. We have now just added payment methods that are popular in different countries.

There are so many touchpoints and everything has taken so much longer than we thought it would to implement. We now spend time on project planning to work out the proper sequence for everything; otherwise, we find we just rework things again and again.

We're just in the process of improving the content on our German and Spanish website now that we've done it in English. We attempted to automate the translation, but as it is so specialist, it didn't really work. Some of the content can be translated automatically, like the product titles, as they are a standard format. But now we're investing in human translation, which can cost about £40,000 for each language as there are so many products, but it is worth the initial investment as the return we will get over three years will run into millions of pounds.

**Interview with Patrick Coghlan,
CEO and Founder, Renovo International**

www.renovointernational.com

The progression of Renovo has been on a trial and error learning curve, like it must be for many forward-thinking businesses. Specifically relating to Amazon, we read the whole of the Amazon European vendor manual, which is a 79-page document and to be honest, complying with some elements like barcoding have been really hard work. The first time we processed an Amazon order it took five hours to do just one. Now it takes just a few minutes because we have embraced technology, enabling us to download the orders via a CSV file direct to our database.

It's important as a business to factor in the cost of compliance with Amazon's conditions and potential chargebacks when things don't quite go to plan. We're developing our presence further by taking advantage of Amazon promotions, including Prime Day, Best Buy and Lightning Deals to help develop Renovo sales further.

Step 6: Get Performing

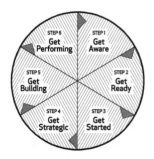

| **GET PERFORMING** |
| Launch |
| Sell |
| Review |

Once you're in **Step 6: Get Performing**, you've done all the hard work! But it is not the end of the story, nor the end of my method. Many companies sit back at this point and expect to see both the leads and sales roll in. While it might have been like that many years ago, it is now important to launch your digital sales channel, then grab your clients' attention and keep running campaigns to attract a constant stream of customers to your digital sales platforms who want to buy or get a quote from you.

Once the new digital sales channels are up and running (whether they are a website, online store, e-marketplace or social store), you will need to work on your visibility to attract traffic and visitors and be the one that is seen and loved, in amongst all the noise of the digital world. Therefore, you will need to manage your digital sales channel closely and do regular reviews to find ways to continually improve sales and gain the return on investment that you've been working towards. This is when you start to reap the rewards from all the work in Steps 1 to 5.

Step 6: Get Performing is actually a step that never ends.

Tasks to Get Performing

Step 6: Get Performing involves the following tasks:
Launch, Sell and Review.

LAUNCH

The main question that you want to answer is: **How do I get my new digital sales channel in front of my potential customers in this country?**

Once your new digital sales channel is ready, you will need to create a buzz around it! This is where you need to employ a whole host of digital marketing techniques and also look for opportunities for offline marketing to get your new digital sales channel out into the digital world, in front of customers all over the world.

There is a whole range of digital marketing and traditional marketing approaches that you can take to drive traffic to your online stores, which will be different for different businesses, depending on whether you are selling products or services, or whether you are selling to customers or other businesses.

Traditionally, SEO was the most important digital marketing technique and it still is important to build it into your website build, e-marketplace listing set up and social selling platform. The majority of the companies I work with still get most of their website traffic through organic search, so SEO is certainly not dead yet. Having good, relevant and enticing copy with relevant keywords that answer the questions your visitors will ask is a top priority. Optimised, relevant images will help your visibility in search engines, e-marketplaces and on social media. As technology continues to develop, you will need to embrace both video optimisation and voice optimisation.

One of the most popular ways of launching online in a new country is to pay for advertising on a search engine, social media platform or online marketplace, which can quickly and very successfully drive new customers to your new digital sales channels. You will have to invest in this with hard cash upfront, although many companies are resistant to do so. You have to make your products and services stand out amongst the millions of search engine listings, the millions of products on an online marketplace or the millions of posts on a social media platform. You may look at starting an e-newsletter, which is a great way of keeping in touch with international customers or you could set up a social media campaign (without paying for advertising).

The Magic 7

It is important to have a website that comes up in a Google search, as I have explained above, but that in itself is not enough. Analysis on Think With Google[44] clearly shows that you need the interaction between multiple different digital marketing channels to drive traffic and online sales. On average, each customer needs seven digital touchpoints before they make an online purchase. So a customer who finds your company website through a Google search would count as one touchpoint, coming across you on social media might be another, and then seeing a paid online advert might be another. The point is that although it is super-important to have a great well-optimised website, you cannot rely on just that – you also need to look good elsewhere online, and in as many places as possible, so that potential customers can ratchet up as many interactions with you as quickly as possible.

ACTIVITY: DIGITAL MARKETING CHECKLIST

My book is about digital sales rather than digital marketing. There have been literally hundreds of books written on this topic, so I'm just going to give you a list of some of the important techniques to consider. All of the elements below can drive traffic to your online digital sales platforms and count as digital touchpoints. Depending on your business, you may want to start with different elements. All of them can achieve excellent results, including:

- Blogs and videos
- Search engine optimisation (SEO)
- Social media
- Paid advertising on search engines
- Paid advertising on social media
- Paid advertising on online marketplaces
- E-newsletters or email marketing
- Mobile or SMS marketing
- Digital catalogues
- Online press release
- Online directories
- Online exhibitions
- Bloggers and influencers
- Chat platforms
- Podcasts and webinars
- Live streaming
- Google Shopping
- Price comparison sites.

ACTIVITY: TRADITIONAL MARKETING CHECKLIST

Traditional marketing techniques can be used at this stage to create awareness of your company, product or service amongst your potential customers in your new international market. It is important to get the right balance between all of these techniques and consider what is the best return you are going to get for your budgets. I've listed some ideas to get you started. Think about what would be most useful and cost-effective for your particular business and sector:

- Holding a product or service launch event
- Attending and showing at an exhibition or tradeshow
- Undertaking a PR campaign
- Sending out a mailshot
- Roundtables
- Articles and advertorials in the industry press.

The problem is that many people still build a website and think that is it. That's like having a business card and never handing it out.

Patrick Coghlan, CEO and Founder, Renovo International

SELL

The main question that you want to answer here is: **How can I increase my online sales?**

This is actually the biggest step of all. If you don't actively sell on a day-to-day basis, it would be the equivalent of setting up an office or shop, but never putting any staff in it and never opening it up. Increasing sales needs to be done, day in day out.

On top of your digital sales platforms, you need good processes for following up on online sales and leads, including:

- Responding to enquiries quickly and competently
- Following up on an abandoned cart on your e-commerce website
- Getting feedback and reviews
- Setting an automated reminder to contact a customer again if there has been no response to an email.

Think of different ways to sell online too, including identifying partners who could send you online referrals, setting up an affiliate scheme where other people in similar niches to yours can promote your product online and get a commission for doing so, or alternatively set up a loyalty programme for repeat customers. These are just a few ideas to get you thinking along the right lines.

Many customers do still like to talk to someone at your company before purchasing, and this will be even more likely if it is a sale to another business or a high value purchase. Make sure that you do have a telephone number available for customer enquiries and customer support, as well as some other tools that will make it easier for international customers to contact you directly, like live chat on your website or even a WhatsApp number, Facebook Messenger account or WeChat if you're targeting China. As sales grow, you will definitely need to have a team member that speaks the local language, which can be a freelance linguist to start with. At the very beginning, you can use Google Translate or an equivalent online machine translation service to get the 'gist' of the email or message you've received, but the quality of these services is not perfect (yet) and can lead to misunderstandings of a linguistic and cultural nature, so use them cautiously and not for anything mission critical.

When you sell in other markets around the world, it can actually get easier to attract customers online, because some countries are either not as advanced in developing and optimising their websites or don't have as many products on their online marketplaces. Often their businesses will not be as streamlined as yours with the same efficient processes. You might actually attract and gain customers more easily than you can do at home.

ACTIVITY: SELL CHECKLIST

Do you have a defined online sales process in place?

Do you have an automated sales process to follow up with customers?

Do you have a way of getting repeat purchases from existing clients?

Do you have a team in place dedicated to the online sales function?

Do you have alternative ways for customers to contact you easily from overseas?

Do you have a way of communicating with customers in their own language?

REVIEW

The main question you want to answer here is: **How quickly can I optimise this digital sales channel in this country, so that I can move onto the next one?**

Companies need to monitor and evaluate what is happening with each of their digital sales platforms and digital marketing campaigns on a daily, weekly or at least a monthly basis, depending on the volume of leads and sales. Make sure that you are constantly looking for areas for improvement. The great thing about all the elements of digital sales is that everything can be measured. You can measure exactly what is working and what is not working in real-time, allowing you to quickly adjust your sales platforms or digital marketing campaigns on the fly. There are very sophisticated digital tools out there too, which help you to see exactly which leads are coming onto your website, or heatmaps that show you exactly how people are using your website in their journey to either making a sale or getting in touch with you. There is so much easily accessible data available that enables you to be agile and make very informed decisions.

As you move further and further through your international digital journey, revisit your original research, proposals and plans from both **Step 4: Get Strategic** and **Step 5: Get Building** and then update them with what you have learnt during this iteration, so that you can improve your build for the next country and the next digital channel, thereby creating an ever-improving circle. This is where my Grow Global Method comes into its own. **Copy, paste, adjust.** This is how you start to get the 10x growth in your online international leads and sales and unstoppable international growth.

ACTIVITY: REVIEW CHECKLIST

Keep on top of your digital sales.

- Sign up for additional digital analytics tools, such as Google Analytics, Lead Forensics or SEMRush, for your website

- Regularly review your analytics data at least once a week, if not daily, from all your digital channels, including your website analytics, e-marketplaces sales analytics and social media and shop analytics

- Spot opportunities to continually improve.

How does Get Performing help you on your international digital journey?

Step 6: Get Performing is the pièce de resistance in your international digital journey that makes everything come to life and brings in the revenue. It also jump starts your performance at a higher level as you go for your next country and channel, taking you from **Duplicate** to **Replicate** and **Proliferate**, getting better and faster all the time!

What happens if you miss out the Get Performing step?

It is a shame to come this far and then sell yourself short at this last and crucial stage. I find that many companies just expect their customers to find them online without putting any effort into promoting their new digital sales platform once it is launched. I also know that many companies fall short and don't invest in making sure the whole digital marketing and sales process is as efficient and automated as possible. Although there are lots of analytics tools out there, very few companies bother to look at them and feedback potential improvements into this process as it is replicated for a new country or new channel. In this way, they miss out on opportunities to promote and improve their digital sales and marketing process time and time again.

Interview with Helen Chapman, Founder of Dotty Fish

www.dottyfish.com

I've always used the internet and I'm always thinking of ways to improve. I'm constantly hungry to sell more.

What's worked for us is a three-pronged approach: extending the range in terms of designs and sizes, just selling in more and more countries and finding new online channels.

We put our shoes onto Amazon in the UK and it took off so quickly it was ridiculous. So, we then listed on the European versions of Amazon and got loads and loads of orders, which we weren't expecting at all. We weren't so lucky on Amazon Japan first time round, but we'll revisit that again in a year and I'll be on it and sort it out. We've also come off some online marketplaces as we couldn't sell profitably or the logistics didn't make sense. But we'll just find others – I've already got a long list from our research.

Our team are on Facebook every day and we've built up a huge following there – we do posts, competitions, giveaways, brand collaborations, it's the same with our blogs. We do everything – Google Ads, Facebook Ads, Amazon Ads, Google Shopping, e-newsletters – and keep auditing our visibility in Google, sign up brand ambassadors... lots of campaigns.

I'm always looking at our sales stats on my iPad and I'm slightly obsessive about looking at the dashboard if I'm honest. We have weekly review meetings with the financial controller. You just can't remain stagnant – you have to move with the times. And what's the worst that can happen? I just think that being digital is being ambitious.

Key Points

- ▶ Building a digital and international business is an investment in your future, not a cost to the business

- ▶ There are 6 steps to the Grow Global Method, which when they are followed impeccably can get you to unstoppable international digital growth

- ▶ The 6 steps are: **Get Aware, Get Ready, Get Started, Get Strategic, Get Building, Get Performing**

- ▶ Do each step fully in order and don't miss any out at all to get the best results

- ▶ The final three steps, **Get Strategic, Get Building** and **Get Performing,** will need repeating for every combination of country and digital sales channel that you select

- ▶ Grab the low-hanging fruit in countries near or similar to yours

- ▶ Put plans in place to do business with more distant and challenging countries over time.

Resources

If you'd like to find out more about how to get this unstoppable international digital growth, check out **www. growglobal.com/growfast** for bonus content. You might like to:

Take a look at my further reading list

Join one of my free webinars or Facebook Lives

Sign up to my online courses, which contain instructions, templates, downloadable activities and a resource section on how exactly to implement each digital sales channel impeccably

Join one of my accelerator programmes, Get World Class or Grow Global, to achieve more international online sales in the fastest possible time, guided by me (see more in the What Next? section).

Chapter 6
Building An International Website

Customers are four times more likely to buy from a website in their own language

IDC[45]

Website visitors stay for twice as long if a website is in their own language

Forrester Research[45]

A lot of companies get overwhelmed when they reach **Step 5: Get Building**, as there seems to be so much to do. My advice is to break it down into manageable chunks and take it bit by bit. In some respects, building your international website is the most important thing you will do, because if you get this right you will have created your own steady stream of international customers. As I've said before, online search accounts for a lot of business, so you need to make sure that Google is finding your website and it is serving up great content to prospective customers. Because this is such a key step, I want to give you some extra advice in addition to what I have covered in **Step 5: Get Building** to make sure that you really nail this. So, in this chapter I will give you some bonus practical insight into precisely what you need to do to build your international digital sales platform successfully, especially your website or e-commerce website, which is a much more complex undertaking.

This is the approach I would suggest you take over time, so it doesn't become totally overwhelming at the start and stop you from even getting started:

- Make it fully international
- Replicate it for speakers of your language in different countries
- Make it multilingual in different languages
- Localise it by adapting it for different countries.

Always bear in mind when you are thinking about your customers: **Which country am I targeting? Which language speakers am I targeting?**

Take It International

Before you can even think about taking your current website into other countries, it is crucial that it's really top-notch as I laid out in **Step 2: Get Ready** and then revisited during your audit in **Step 3: Get Started.** This gives you a strong foundation from which to sell to customers all around the world. A happy side effect of carrying out this work is that your online business will increase in your home country too.

For my examples, I will refer to the UK as the home territory but the principle is universal, irrespective of what country you are in.

Next, make sure your website is open for business from international visitors, but is still written in your home language.

It would be good to move to a .com domain name at this point (if you haven't already or don't have another top-level domain name like .net). By having a top-level domain name (as opposed to a country-specific domain name, like .co.uk), you will be more visible on search engines all around the world, and more likely to attract more international customers to your website. However, if you already have a high-performing website that is not on a .com website, the process of moving to a .com has to be handled with extreme care, so that you can maintain your current website traffic volumes as much as possible. By moving away from a country-specific domain name, you may experience a small reduction in traffic in your home country, but it should be more than offset by the increase in international traffic you will benefit from. You might decide to keep your local country website too, but there are lots of factors that you need to consider and it's likely you will need some help in making that decision.

Website

There are small low-cost changes you can start to make so that it looks like you are open for business internationally, like putting your telephone number with an international dialling code or testimonials from clients in other countries. If you are a service company, you can say 'we work with clients all around the world', and feature case studies from any iconic projects you have carried out or add press coverage you have received in other countries.

E-commerce

Start to add some indicators on your website so that customers know you welcome international visitors, such as putting 'we ship internationally' or adding other currencies. Companies usually start in their local currency, euros and dollars, and also add globally recognised payment methods, like PayPal or Amazon Payments.

Most people get to this stage and then say that their website is international and stop there. But there is so much more that can be done to adapt your website for international visitors.

Replicate It in the Same Language

Next, set up your website or e-commerce site and actively go in search of new customers who speak the same language as you. This works particularly well for your business if you are lucky enough to be a speaker of a world language, like English, French,

Spanish, Arabic or Russian. In this way, you can very quickly reuse content you have already created in your home language for new customers in other countries. There are so many things to think about when you go international, it is actually safer to start off in your own language. Then, at least you can offer a seamless customer service, albeit it might be at a different time of day.

So, for example, if you are going to keep your websites in English, you can start to reach English-speaking international customers in Ireland, the USA, Canada, South Africa, Australia and New Zealand, as well as in countries where English is widely spoken, such as India, some African and Caribbean countries, as well as Hong Kong and Singapore.

> *Given that nearly 325 million people live in the USA, compared to about 65 million in the UK, businesses from the UK targeting the USA can have a potential market five times bigger than their home market.*

To do this right, a good option is to add dedicated pages to your .com site for each country you are targeting. So, if your website is abc.com and you want to target customers in New Zealand, set up a section dedicated to New Zealand at abc.com/nz, and if you are targeting Australia, it would be abc.com/au. I call these country mini-sites, 'hanging off' the main .com.

Alternatively, you can set up completely separate local country websites, so you would have a website for New Zealand called abc.co.nz or for Australia it would be abc.com.au. Some local country domains are open for everyone to buy. However, some are a little trickier to get hold of. For example, you currently need a registered trademark or registered company name to register in Australia.

There are many behind the scenes technical tasks that you need to do to get your website set up correctly to make sure your website or mini-sites are visible in search engines internationally, as well as to ensure that the right language version of your website appears in the right version of Google or any other search engine.

A company making bespoke luxury swimming pools selected the USA as their first market to tackle. Their market research showed that they should, in fact, focus their efforts on just the East Coast, as the whole country was too big to take on in one go. They chose to have a .com website for the USA and keep their .co.uk website for the UK, as they were only offering a subset of their services in America due to the distance.

Make It Multilingual

The next step is to replicate and actively go in search of new customers that speak other languages for your website and e-commerce site. Can you imagine if you were faced with a Chinese website in the local renminbi currency – would you buy from it if you didn't speak Chinese? So you need to put yourself in the shoes of all these potential international customers and think about how they might feel buying from, say, a .co.uk website in English and in pounds sterling. What can you do in order to make them feel as comfortable buying from your website as they would buying from one in their own country?

Having web pages with content in the local language will mean that you appeal to customers in different countries and can be more visible in local versions of the search engines.

So, if you are going to make your website multilingual, which languages are the best to start with? With around 200 countries and 6,800 languages in the world, it is clear that you cannot target them all at once.

I suggest going for the world languages first – that is the most spoken languages around the world, which are spoken in multiple countries. English, Mandarin Chinese, Spanish, Portuguese French, German, Arabic, Russian might all be on your list, depending on where there is demand for your products and services and how easy it is to do business in those countries (you worked on this in **Step 3: Get Started**, the Feasibility task).

If you put a page on your website, in say Spanish, it might be that it would appear in search engines in Mexico and Argentina, as well as in Spain – and there are 21 Spanish-speaking markets in total. This is where my 6-step method becomes so powerful, as you gain new customers from all over the world with much less effort and maximising your return on the original investment in translation.

> *A company who provided high class accessories for first class airplane cabins decided to translate about five pages of their website into Spanish, detailing their company overview and main products. Within three months, they secured a $50,000 order from an airline in Latin America, which had seen its listing in Google while in Colombia. The profit from this order more than paid for their initial investment in their website, its translation and localisation.*

When structuring your website for multiple languages, it is a little more complex.

You can set up a dedicated local website e.g. abc.es for Spain in Spanish, abc.de for Germany in German (this is the Amazon approach). Alternatively, you can set up mini country sites which effectively hang off your main .com website e.g. abc.com/es for Spain in Spanish, abc.com/de for Germany in German (this is the Apple approach). There is one more option if you are going to sell widely in multilingual countries. For example, you would set up abc.com/ca/en for Canada in the English language or abc.com/ca/fr for Canada in the French language (this is the Ikea approach).

Without getting too complicated, if you are a service company and want to attract all Spanish speakers, then it is possible to set up a website abc.com/es to appeal to all Spanish language speakers, without targeting it to one particular country version of Google. This means that, in this instance, you would not target your website to Spain only, as you'd actually like that part of your website to be visible to customers in all Spanish-speaking countries. Many businesses use the 'Apple' approach, and while it does depend on your business type and business structure, it can save you money on buying multiple domains for each country. However, I would suggest that you buy them anyway to protect your brand name, even if you don't use them. In some countries, customers are more used to seeing a .fr website, but you have to balance that against the fact that if you do go for a separate .fr website, you are effectively starting again with a brand new website. This can take time to get established in the search engines from a standing start.

You would still use essentially the same look and feel at this stage – the same branding, design, layout and images. You need to translate all navigation tabs, buttons and any text on images, as well as all the terms and conditions and other content you generally find in a website footer.

Again, there are a host of behind the scenes technical tasks you need to do to make sure that your website or mini-sites are visible internationally and to make sure that the right language version of your website appears in the right version of Google, or any other search engine, and that you do not end up with duplicate content. Things start to get a lot more complex from this point forward, as you are managing another version of your content in a language that you may not even speak. You must use professional translators to get these translations done, rather than rely on machine translation, like Google Translate. I would always recommend that you use a professional translator, even if you have a team member who speaks the language for two reasons: one they are not a professional translator (just because I am an English speaker, does not mean I am a copywriter) and they are better off doing the job they are employed and paid to do, rather than translating. Basically, leave the translation to the translators.

You will need language speakers available to your business to do this really well, so a good plan is to internationalise your website alongside a plan to hire language speakers to build up your in-house language capability, or if you are just starting off and don't yet have demand for a full-time language speaker, to work with a freelance speaker of that particular language on an as-needed basis. This is critical as you will need to fully service these clients and the best way to do this is in their own language.

A legal firm had a plan to attract more international clients onto its books. It took a very clear approach, translating its website into Spanish at the same time as recruiting a Spanish lawyer, who was also qualified in English law and fluent in both English and Spanish. The number of clients from the Spanish-speaking world increased quickly and the next year, they replicated this approach by recruiting a bilingual French-English solicitor.

Make It Local

Finally, take the internationalisation one step further by adapting the content to appeal to your target markets and customers, creating specific content that is more culturally relevant to them and their preferences.

> *A client was selling products into the sports market. Very popular sports featured heavily on his UK website, such as football, rugby and cricket, while his Irish website led with Gaelic dancing and hurling, and his French website had handball products. This website was pulling off the same basic product database, but what he chose to display was different for each country, depending on his customers' preferences for different sports.*

Website

There are many things that need to be adapted or localised on your website. These range from changing spellings, terminology and tone of voice, even for different versions of English: 'trousers' becomes 'pants', 'jewellery' is 'jewelry' and 'pyjamas' changes to 'pajamas'. It's not just retail goods that change their names – 'aluminium' morphs into the shorter 'aluminum'.

Images are also important. As they say, 'a picture paints a thousand words' and gives a visual cue to your international visitors, without the need for words to get your message across, transcending language. Images, in particular, need to be updated to reflect local cultures and local environments. A street in London looks completely different to one in Chicago. The same applies to videos and animations.

Also, different cultures communicate in different ways and have different preferences. A Chinese website often looks really busy to an untrained Western eye, where a lot of 'white space' is preferred and there is a 'less is more' mentality. Messages themselves will need updating too. Some cultures are very direct and transactional, like the USA where you are more likely to see strong selling messages, whereas in Japan you are likely to see more relationship-building type content that is understated. This is a great opportunity to write blogs for different audiences and send e-newsletters with targeted local messages.

E-commerce

When you're selling products internationally, you may have to localise your products or services in different countries. Some of these include:

- Regulations/certifications e.g. fire safety for furniture, FDA approval for foods and supplements, accountants qualifying in local country
- Size of product e.g. cushions are bulky vs. cushion covers, which can be easily posted
- Weight of products e.g. bulky furniture, large machinery
- Restrictions e.g. some metals can't be imported, shipping liquids like beer or wine
- Updating product guarantees and return policies to fit with local legislation
- Local currencies, payment systems, sales taxes, shipping costs and methods, as well as customs duties.

Selling products online also attracts additional costs, including:

- Payment method fees
- International delivery
- Processing returns

- Regulations, compliance & certification costs
- Local language labels
- Local language packaging
- Warehousing & fulfilment
- Customs duties.

 Key Points

▸ It gets more complex to build an international, multilingual and localised digital sales platform, so do it bit by bit

▸ Work out if your business is targeting countries or language speakers or both

▸ It is critical to choose the correct technical structure for your international website right from the start so that you can get the full advantage of internationalising

▸ Translate and localise product and service information for online marketplaces and social media selling, although your online partners will do this in their countries.

 Resources

If you'd like to find out more about how to do this properly, check out **www.growglobal.com/growfast** to access my online courses.

Chapter 7
Getting It Right

Firms must take a different approach to digital strategy, embedding digital capabilities into the heart of their businesses, rather than treating digital touchpoints as peripheral add-ons. They must become lean, agile and digitally savvy.

Enhance Your Digital Capabilites, Forrester[46]

Now you have a good handle on what needs to be done and in what order, I'd like to share with you a few insider tips and tricks you can utilise while successfully implementing your digital growth strategy.

In this chapter, I'm going to run through the key things that you can do to give yourself the best chance of success, based upon what my best-performing clients have done. I'm also going to outline some common pitfalls to avoid. These are the stumbling blocks I have seen companies of all sizes struggle with. These mistakes really hold companies back, which is such a shame when there is so much opportunity out there.

You are in it for the long haul. Do it this way and you will gain the full results you deserve and grow truly globally. You really can't afford to miss out. The digital age is already here. So, let's get you off to the best start...

Are you ready to get it right?

Top 6 Success Factors for Digital Global Growth

Having worked with a real range of businesses, both in terms of size and sector, I have noticed that these are the 6 most important elements you need to get right. Take a close look at any company that is doing well internationally, and they will have mastered them all.

Tip 1. Embrace New Opportunities

You have to be aware of the potential opportunities out there for your business and be hungry enough to go after them. You need to be open to change. There is no telling just how much international digital sales could elevate your company's profits. I have been working with a set of pioneering companies who have managed to forge ahead and made selling online around the world not only a reality, but also the core of their businesses. They have changed their whole business models and now use digital sales as the main tool to generate international leads and sales, often moving away from traditional agent, distributor, stockists or retailer models in the process. This is truly game-changing, and has meant they've already surpassed the expectations of what they thought was possible for their company.

You need to be prepared to shake things up. Resistance to change always kills innovation, so make sure that the key decision makers in your business are on board and ready for this international adventure.

It will be a rewarding experience as you will learn new digital skills and do business with people from all over the world. You will get a huge amount of satisfaction when you see the fruits of your work pay off as your business starts to grow globally and it brings financial rewards to both you and your business.

Tip 2. Think carefully and strategically

In order to successfully grow your international business, your digital strategy needs to be part of the fabric of your business. You will need to think holistically about the whole business and not just treat digital as an add-on. It's so much more than 'just building a website'.

Many traditional companies don't get to the **Dedicate** stage of my international digital journey or place emphasis on digital until they hit about a $1 million turnover, although many think about going international before this, usually in response to enquiries or sales that land at their feet. They become what we call 'accidental exporters'.

At this point, some businesses react by undertaking tactical tasks. They often jump from task to task at random or copy competitors without giving it any real thought. This is a disjointed approach that is based on a hunch, not a strategic approach based on research with a coherently thought out plan.

If you don't take global growth seriously and fail to give it the resources it needs, you are not going to see significant returns. I have seen lots of businesses get stuck in the **Deviate** or **Orientate** stage of my international digital journey, where they are not really committed to digital or international growth and so don't allocate the resources it needs to truly take off. In this scenario, the person in charge of implementing the strategy does so with one arm tied behind their back. They cannot deliver the growth they would like to because they have not been fully equipped to do so.

This doesn't have a happy ending. When things don't work out as planned, people either quickly get stuck or they slip back into the **Procrastinate** stage of the international digital journey when they don't see the results they had hoped for and lose momentum.

As a result, they lose the support of the board, or at least the marketing or sales director, and end up with their budgets being diverted elsewhere. This is a waste of the time and money that's already been invested, but the biggest waste of all is they miss out on the opportunity to sell online around the world.

Tip 3. Be prepared to invest

Global growth does not come cheap. If you want to grow fast, you have to be prepared to commit to some investment.

But what if you invest $5,000 and get $50,000 back?

What if you invest $50,000 and get $500,000 back?

Our wisest clients are now asking this question: What do I have to invest, and where do I have to invest it to bring in $1 million of increased online international sales? These are the companies who are going to set themselves apart and forge their paths in the online world across the globe. They have a truly global mindset.

Global growth can be explosive. In fact, you can double your online turnover in 12 months. I have seen companies do that at all stages of growth in all industries of all sizes, but it requires that you make initial investment to kick-start the process. You need to allocate a budget to cover the work that you need to do in order to build a new digital sales channel in another country. But remember, this figure will be a lot less than the ongoing cost of having a sales manager or attending overseas exhibitions.

So, you need to change your mindset from thinking about how much it costs to what this investment will bring you in return. Bust the myths and allow your business to seize the opportunity that selling online around the world presents.

Tip 4. Pick the winners

Take an honest look at your entire product or service range and see if it is really something that is truly different, unique, or best in class, that will be in demand from international customers. If you don't have anything really different, then you will need to compete on price or customer service instead, or put a lot more investment into creating a desirable brand in your target country. This has to be something that I call a 'superlative' product or service: the best, the oldest, the fastest, the newest, the only...

Tip 5. Get the right team

You need to make sure you have exactly the right blend of skills for the job, so don't just settle for the first person that comes across your radar. You may find that there is no one currently within your company that offers what you need. If so, you will need to look outside to either freelancers or agencies. Be realistic about what your needs are and the potential skills gap in your company. Then bring in the people who have both the experience and expertise to make your global growth happen. It may seem expensive to start with, but having the right people in place will enable you to achieve your goal much faster. As you grow, you will need an experienced and capable project manager who keeps everybody on track and working together. It can make or break your project. The biggest companies in the world have a Digital Director, as you can't become a more digital company without the right people leading the charge[47]. Take the lead from these big corporates and adapt this practice for your own business. Also, be honest with yourself – do you have the capacity to implement and manage an additional digital sales channel in another country right now? It is OK to put the idea on the backburner for a while until you are really ready to go for it.

Tip 6. Get professional help to speed up progress

For over five years, I've helped clients to get it right. If you get help at the right points, it maintains the momentum of the project and you can then surge up through the international digital journey. If you get an expert to help you put a world-class digital presence in place at the **Dedicate** stage, you will grow globally very quickly at the **Duplicate** stage.

It is a strength to look outside your organisation and get help from experts who live and breathe best practice, drawing it from all those businesses who are experimenting at the forefront of the field. If you can be told what works and what doesn't – you will move faster and with more certainty. With me guiding you through the whole of the Grow Global Method via my online courses or dedicated programmes, you'll achieve your business' strategic goals and international ambitions, and get the results you need fast.

The 4 Biggest Pitfalls To Avoid

I have seen many businesses fail to gain the benefits they deserve due to these four simple pitfalls. It is so sad to see because they can completely derail international digital growth, and yet every one of them is totally avoidable. So please take heed and pay particular attention to each of these things, so you that I don't see you make the same mistakes.

Pitfall 1. Poor tech

Poor tech will undermine the whole sales process and your ability to really scale up. A lot of companies start out on the wrong digital sales platforms because they get the cheapest they can or one that a friend's friend has recommended. This inevitably leads to throwing good money after bad. There are companies that continue to upgrade and tweak a poorly built website, which has never really worked for them and is not built to best practice.

This leaves them vulnerable to technical hitches that can throw a project into crisis, whether that is the website going down, or a search engine or e-marketplace algorithm update that means they start to lose customers. They realise too late that their current website is either not able to go international, or if it can, it will require great expense or a lot of custom work. It can only get the business so far and so isn't a launchpad to take them fully international. So make sure you are fully equipped from the start.

Pitfall 2. Messy back office

Companies always overlook the importance of getting the back office systems in place so that they are ready to scale once the fast international growth takes off. I know it might not be the most exciting part of your business, but if you don't have smooth operations, systems and logistics, you'll soon end up under strain. Even worse, you will either end up firefighting and letting customers down, or in the best-case scenario, not keep up with the speed of growth. Don't limit yourself in this way, make sure that your systems can handle a surge in sales before you start driving them.

Pitfall 3. Lazy localising

It is inexcusable to believe that everyone will be able to speak your language, or if they do speak another language, will be happy to use Google Translate to navigate their way through your website – that's just lazy. Companies that do think this way will miss out on big opportunities to add local contact details, have customer service representatives available at different times of the day, or even add local currencies and payment methods.

Customers will respond better to you and buy more if you localise your digital presence for them. I'm not saying that you need to have hundreds of dedicated websites and languages, but once you have established which languages are important to your business, create some dedicated content for that language-speaking audience before your competitors do. One size does not fit all.

Pitfall 4. Thinking you're done

It is wrong to think that the sales will start flowing in when a website is launched or a product is put up on an e-marketplace. There are impatient companies who pull the plug without giving it sufficient time to succeed or without supporting their new digital sales channel with the digital marketing that is needed to gain traction.

Launching a new digital sales channel is really exciting, of course, but you will need to actively build up traffic and sales over time. Otherwise, it's the equivalent of having a beautiful shop stocked with great products tucked away where no one will ever find it. I hate to see companies that have put the energy into launching a new channel, only to let it go flat because they have no digital marketing plan to drive traffic towards it.

Other companies can get complacent. Initially, they are happy with the boost there is in sales or leads, but then wonder why they plateau. Such companies can build amazing websites that are full of great products and services, only to lose interest in keeping them up-to-date. The truth is, that is not enough to establish your international digital presence and make online sales. You also need to encourage previous clients to come back to you with promotions and interesting and engaging things to read, listen or watch. Otherwise, what was the point in building the platform in the first place?

Growth Myths

Finally, if you believe any of these things, then you and your global growth mission will fail. It is incredible how often I hear these myths:

1. My son's friend's cousin can build my website for me.

2. Once my new website is built, that'll be it for 5 years. I can just sit back and watch the money roll in.

3. My marketing intern who speaks Spanish can run my international e-commerce website.

4. I don't need to put my e-marketplace listings into German, as everyone in Germany understands English.

5. I'm only doing social media because my competitors are, but really I think it is a waste of time.

6. My web company guarantee that they will get me to Number 1 on Google.

You have been warned!

Key Points

▸ Despite great guidance, some companies still ignore game-changing advice

▸ You have to start right, invest right, hire right and don't be afraid to ask for help

▸ Avoid bad tech choices and don't rush in. Do not offer a one-size-fits-all solution, get complacent or give up.

THE DIGITAL FUTURE. ARE YOU GETTING LEFT BEHIND?

The world has changed because of the new technology. In the future, there will be no Made In China, no Made in America, no Made in Peru. It's going to be made on the internet. [It will] enable every small business to buy global, sell globally, deliver globally, pay globally and travel globally. This is the trend, nobody can stop it.

Jack Ma, Alibaba, World Economic Forum, Davos 2018[48]

Now that you've got to the end of this book, you will no doubt have realised that you have a lot to do to transform your business so that you can compete in today's international and digital world. You may feel that you're already behind the times and need to play catch up in this digital age.

The exciting part is how much potential growth is waiting for you. The technology just keeps on evolving and the opportunity just keeps on growing with it. You have to grow faster: in your know-how, insight, skills and implementation. You can't rest on your laurels at all – there just isn't the time. You have to take this seriously and take action now. If you can't keep up today, then you are going to really struggle with what's coming tomorrow.

In Part C, I'm going to show you what is just around the corner in the digital future that will have an impact on selling online internationally. The digital future is another whole book in itself! It is not my intention to overwhelm you. Instead, I hope to give you an incentive to make sure that you act as soon as you finish reading this book. If you have any teammates who aren't fully on board with mission digital, then there is plenty of information in the next few pages that will make them change their mind.

Are you changing fast enough to face the digital future?

Chapter 8
The International Digital Future

What we need to do is always lean into the future, when the world changes around you and when it changes against you – what used to be a tail wind is now a head wind – you have to lean into that and figure out what to do.

Jeff Bezos, Amazon[49]

As we move towards 2020, the velocity of technological change is unprecedented. Your business must learn how to keep up with and embrace change, so that you don't become irrelevant and unprofitable. It may sound dramatic, but that is the reality you face.

In this chapter, I will give you a whistle-stop tour of some of the headlines and innovations. These may seem a little sci-fi at the moment, but they are tipped to become mainstream before you know it. Developing an awareness and understanding of how these innovations are going to shake things up as you grow globally will give you an advantage over your competitors. Unfortunately, these technological trends are not Star Trek-esque pipe dreams – they are reality right now. It is predicted the pace of change in technology in the next five years will be unprecedented. So you really do need to act now or be left behind.

Are You Ready For What's Coming Next?

These four trends are going to change our international digital world over the next five years, so you should be mindful of them while building any sort of international growth plan.

- **Online users will boom.** There are ambitious projects to bring internet access to everyone in the world. This will be mainly in remote areas of the developing world, but the boom will also meet the increased demand there is in big cities, which means it's predicted that 5 billion more people will be online. Not only that, but the world's population is growing rapidly, so our future markets will be different. The demographics will be different too: there will be a much younger population in some countries, a much older one in others and a growing middle class that has money in their pockets in other nations. This will mean that nearly all your potential customers across the whole world will be online.

- **Mobile will be mainstream.** The number of people using the internet on their phones, as well as browsing for products and services and making purchases, will grow enormously. Mobile is expected to become the main way for all of us to connect. This will change the way that you interact with your customers online, and the way they want to interact with you. It will also impact the way that payments are made online.

- **The digital landscape will change.** Digital players in the international market will consolidate and evolve. Some will even die and new game-changers will be born. New digital sales channels will emerge that allow you to reach new international customers in new ways, like v-commerce and c-commerce. Make sure that you are in a position to capitalise on this.

- **Technology will become more sophisticated.** Technology will offer new and exciting efficiencies for your business. Transaction technology will make payments across different currencies smoother and provide a better user experience. Translation technology will also make it easier for you to create content and communicate with customers in other languages.

Even More People Will Be Online

Internet coverage will boom worldwide

Analysts are now split on how things are going to move forward with the growth of internet usage. One estimate is that nearly all the world's 8 billion people will be online by 2020, and another is that just 4 billion will be[50].

The most optimistic predictions are based upon the development of technology coming on leaps and bounds, much of which sounds quite sci-fi. But it's not! There are four competing projects to connect the whole of the world's population to the internet in the next 10 years by using a host of different techniques (Google's X's Project Loon, Facebook's Connectivity Lab with Aquila, Tesla's Elon Musk with Space X and Virgin's Richard Branson with OneWeb). These range from a network of balloons travelling in the stratosphere to solar-powered gliders taking to the skies.

On the other hand, some analysts predict there will be a slowdown in the growth of internet users because of the same problem that the technology giants are trying to resolve – developing countries still do not have internet access in their more remote regions, and this is becoming increasing difficult to implement by building the broadband and satellite infrastructure that is needed. Satellite internet is already very well established and offers increasingly fast connection rates across the world as new technology becomes available.

What does this mean for you now?

As more and more people come online, you should plan to work in multiple languages in the future as I believe we will reach a tipping point where more people and businesses will publish content on the internet in their own language.

Billions of new customers in new corners of the world

The world's population is going to rise from 7.5 billion to nearly 10 billion by 2050[51]. This enormous increase is incredible, and it's also amazing where these new customers are expected to be located:

- In Asia, the population will be over 5 billion (over half the world's population)
- In Africa, the population will double to 2.5 billion (a quarter of the world's population)
- In the Americas, the population will be just over 1 billion (just a modest increase)
- Europe will have a population of about 0.7 billion (this means it is actually in decline)
- Oceania's population will double to 66 million.

India's population is expected to overtake China's in 2024, and Nigeria will become the world's third largest country before 2050, overtaking the USA[52].

Half of the world's population growth will be concentrated in just nine countries: India, Nigeria, the Democratic Republic of the Congo, Pakistan, Ethiopia, the United Republic of Tanzania, the USA, Uganda and Indonesia[51].

By 2050, the biggest countries by GDP are expected to be: China, USA, India, Indonesia, Japan, Brazil, Germany, Mexico, the United Kingdom and Russia. However, some of the biggest GDP growth[53] will be in: Iraq, Ethiopia, Uzbekistan, Nepal, Côte d'Ivoire, Iceland, Laos and Bangladesh. Therefore, the purchasing power is shifting from Western economies to Eastern economies.

There will be billions of new customers in Asia and Africa, who will mostly be in a much younger age group. This will mirror the trend found in Uganda, where for example, 70% of the population is under 25[54]. In contrast, traditionally strong economies, like Japan and most of Europe, will have an ageing population. Asia already has over 500 million middle class people, which is more than the European Union's total population. Over the next two decades, the middle class is expected to expand by another three billion. They will come almost exclusively from the emerging economies[9].

The e-commerce customers of the future will be from different places too. The largest e-commerce economies by 2050 are expected to be: China, Malaysia, Bolivia, Kenya, Russia, Turkey, Saudi Arabia, Bangladesh, Colombia and the UAE[55], which is so different from the biggest economies of today.

What does this mean for you now?

You will have the potential to reach millions of new customers in new places around the world, so it is critical that you start to make plans to do business in these new countries now. As purchasing power rises, these nations will be definite potential markets for your products and services if you are an early mover. Think carefully about your target demographic and where there is the most opportunity for growth e.g. if you offer a luxury good you will want to focus on countries where there is a boom in middle-class people. As this is unchartered territory, make sure you get help in identifying countries that could be hotspots for your products and services in the future, so that you can beat your competitors to them.

Mobile Will Be Mainstream

The move to mobile use is unrelenting, as the world has moved to 'mobile first'. Most new users will access the internet through their mobile. This, in fact, will be the only way they connect.

Connections are getting faster in most countries around the world using 3G and 4G, with the new 5G also becoming commercially available soon. However, nearly 30% of the world's online population are still accessing via 2G[24]. Some analysts predict that there will be a slowdown in the growth of the number of mobile users as the limits of geography and technology are met. But with the introduction of new handsets in India for as low as $7[56], it seems that more and more people will have access to the internet.

Mobile online payment methods are developing quickly with new entrants to the market now appearing in different parts of the world, especially Asia and Africa. China has AliPay, WeChat Pay and TenPay mobile apps, which have been a big driver in the rapid uptake of e-commerce in the country. Innovations in mobile 'banking' in Africa and peer-to-peer bankless payment systems are leading the way worldwide, like M-PESA in Kenya. Nearly two-thirds of the Kenyan population use this service, yet less than 5% have a credit card[57].

What does this mean for you now?

You need to consider how you communicate with your new customers through mobile. It is a good idea to both provide content that can be viewed on low bandwidth internet connections and offer a larger variety of payment methods for e-commerce and m-commerce if you are selling online and through mobile.

The Digital Landscape Will Change

Future of search

Search is moving rapidly beyond just text search. Image search, video search and now voice search are all becoming more important (see more in the V-commerce section below). New visual search engines are being developed that will bring knowledge of the internet to millions of people with a low level of literacy. Google Lens and Pinterest Lens are emerging as market leaders, as well as the e-commerce giants Amazon, Walmart and ASOS. This technology allows you to search for a product by taking a photo on your mobile phone[58]. Google and YouTube both have massive video search engines and developments in the technology that will make it even easier to search the content of a video, even when a transcript or subtitles are not included.

What does this mean for you now?

You will have to adapt the type of online content you have and the way you present it in order to make it visible on these alternative search tools. Although it may be hard to imagine how customers would be able to search for your products or services without typing in words, this development could actually make it easier for you to go international, as images and videos can remove any problematic language barriers.

Future of e-marketplaces

For those of you selling products, it is expected that e-marketplaces will see a lot of consolidation, with some of the smaller country players and vertical players being taken over, and possibly four to six of the biggest e-marketplaces becoming global players (Amazon, Ebay, NewEgg, Rakuten, Tmall and JD.com are already global). The big companies are also taking shares in smaller national and regional marketplaces or buying them out completely, as has happened with Amazon and Souq.com in the Middle East. The winners in this race to e-commerce dominance will be the companies with the price, range and speed of delivery, as well as trust and good service.

However, there are still some big newcomers who are yet to enter centre stage and will no doubt shake things up. Facebook marketplace is rolling out globally, marketing itself as people-to-people commerce and allowing you to connect via Messenger, where you can also pay.

What does this mean for you now?

It is becoming more and more difficult to become visible in the big online marketplaces, so companies will have to invest in a larger budget to pay-to-play and may face frequent rule changes. This means sellers will always be vulnerable to the barriers of increased cost and gaining visibility[59], especially in the big marketplaces like Amazon and Tmall.

New digital sales channels

Watch out for the new emerging digital sales channels and be an early adopter, giving yourself the freedom to experiment with them.

Online sales funnels

Another new emerging digital sales channel is the use of digital sales funnels. The aim is to take new customers through a value ladder of products or services as they become more interested in what you do. This is essentially like a website with logic built in, and depends on the action that a customer takes on the step before. A sales funnel is an online sales tool that entices you in via an offer that you sign up for. After you give them your email address, they take you through what is essentially an online sales script to upsell more products and services to you. They will keep in contact with you, luring you in closer and closer to the sale by presenting targeted offers to you.

Two market leaders are ClickFunnels and LeadPages. For services, you can offer an expert white paper for free and then upsell them to join a webinar or book an online consultation with you. For products, you may offer a free gift or sample, and then upsell to a larger quantity or a complimentary product.

With an online sales funnel, you don't actually need a website at all, as your customers can take bookings and make purchases from the funnel. This could actually be the start of a post-website era.

What does this mean for you now?

Although these digital sales funnels are becoming more widely used, they are still in their infancy. So experiment now as it will require a lot of trial and error or A/B testing before you can perfect the ideal funnel for your particular customers. The good thing is that once you master these funnels, they can be easily duplicated into other languages, enabling you to target potential customers in other countries quite precisely.

C-commerce

The main story of 2017 was the growth of chat apps. WhatsApp and Facebook Messenger remain the most popular, with 1.3 and 1.2 billion users respectively. China's WeChat has 938 million users and QQ 861 million[19]. Others include Skype, Viber, Snapchat, Line and Telegram, which are all ones to watch as you keep an eye on how the world of chat and messenger apps play out in the future.

Chat apps are used much more extensively in Asia and are replacing email for everyday communication in a business context. But it is their future potential as a digital sales platform to sell to customers all around the world that is really interesting. This is already being named as c-commerce or conversational commerce.

WeChat is leading the way with c-commerce in China, where companies set up accounts and sell using payments like its own

WePay. Facebook Messenger has added payment facilities recently and there will be an evolution of this service over the next few years. With chatbots being developed and put into operation, we might not even need stores or e-commerce websites. Instead, we will have a personal digital shopper, helping us to choose an outfit or guiding us to the best insurance policy through an online automated conversation. As translation technology takes leaps and bounds, we will be able to do this in many different languages.

What does this mean for you now?

Chat apps and c-commerce are again in their infancy, but my first clients are starting to experiment with them and see what is possible. Again, the chatbots of the future will be able to work across languages and make international online sales more than possible.

V-commerce

The advent of new digital assistants, like Alexa (Amazon), Cortana (Microsoft), Siri (Apple), Google Home and Genie (Alibaba) provide another way to sell to customers online around the world. There are others that are emerging, including M (Facebook Messenger), as well as Bixby (Samsung), which means that voice search has already entered our homes. There were about 36 million digital assistants in 2017 and Amazon's Alexa was by far the largest digital assistant with over 70% of the global market share. However, many of its rivals are only just launching theirs[60]. **By 2021, it is predicted there will be more digital assistants than the world's population**, with Google's digital assistants leading the market[61]. Google Assistant is available in over 30 languages and will be extended over time to more and more languages.

China is taking its place too, with all the big digital players each having their own offerings, including Xiaowei (Tencent, who own WeChat), Xiaoyu Zaijia (or Little Fish from Baidu) and DingDong (the big marketplace JD.com). Comscore predicts that 50% of searches will be via voice by 2020.[62]

What does this mean for you now?

The future of voice commerce is still anyone's guess at the moment, but one thing is for sure: it will change the way that that you search and order products and services online across the world. It will have an impact on how you build your primary sales channels too – from your websites to your online marketplace listings. You can experiment with these new digital channels to get an early mover advantage.

Technology Will Be More Sophisticated

Technology advancements that are happening right now will help you to do business more quickly and efficiently with international customers:

- **Artificial Intelligence:** AI is already being integrated into many applications we use daily – whether that be online customer support and customer service or the search algorithms for Google, eBay and Facebook. The possibility of 24/7 first line support for our customers in multiple languages does sound appealing as it will reduce the need for more multilingual customer service representatives as your business grows, as well as reduce your costs while increasing customer satisfaction.

- **Automation:** A business cannot compete today by doing everything manually. The automation of marketing, sales and operations processes will help you to achieve world-class operations, such as running digital marketing campaigns 24 hours a day, 7 days a week and automatically updating your customer relationship management systems and accounts systems.

- **Blockchain:** New blockchain technology is already allowing secure purchase along the whole of the supply chain across borders. It is expected to revolutionise many areas of business, including financial transactions, payments and contracts.

- **Virtual currencies:** There are thousands of digital currencies already in existence with Bitcoin and Ethereum being two of the market leaders. Small and large retailers are already accepting payment by Bitcoin, from Expedia the global online travel agency to Virgin Galactic, if you fancy space travel. It is predicted that both governments and the big technology players, like Facebook and Google, will issue their own digital currencies in the future. Virtual currencies are interesting if you are selling internationally, as they transcend national borders and are effectively a global currency.

- **E-commerce:** The trend is towards personalisation, with businesses tailoring products and services to a market of one. This focuses on how we can adapt to customer's different preferences and buying patterns in different cultures around the world. Consumers will continually switch between their multiple devices e.g. mobile, tablet, desktop computer, digital assistant – and whatever may come next. Back on the high street, their digital behaviour may trigger in-store offers that are tailored just for them, as near field technology takes off. Use of drones and robots will make logistics and delivery a whole new ball game, as well as new global underground distribution hubs in cities like Dubai.

- **New applications:** as our world becomes increasingly complex, there are applications springing up with clever technology that help international businesses to trade online across borders, handle international sales tax, use different payment methods and push our inventory to different international digital sales platforms at the same time.

What does this mean for you now?

The pace of technological change is set to accelerate. This will have an impact on not only how you run your business, but also how you trade with international clients and customers across borders. You have to set aside time in your busy schedules to really understand and evaluate how this technology could be useful to you.

Translation technology talks

Up until now the quality of automatic machine translation has not been accurate enough for me to recommend using it for business websites and marketplace product listings. It has also been a challenge to provide customer service and support to those who speak different languages. However, huge strides are being taken with machine translation. The accuracy and speed at which machines can do translation is improving day-by-day. These systems, from Google Translate to Facebook DeepText, run on machine learning, so they will get better and more accurate over time. In fact, it is reported that they are learning languages even faster than their creators expected and are gaining near-human accuracy[63]. Other amazing innovations include Skype Translator with multilingual video calling, which has introduced a real-time translation facility while on live video chat. This makes language differences almost irrelevant, as well as Google Pixel Buds, which allows real-time translation from your Android phone, almost like a scene from the *Dr Who* TV series.

What does this mean for you now?

There is, of course, still much more work to be done in this area, as more languages are added and the accuracy of translation improves for all languages. The good news for those of you with huge inventories of products or stacks of articles on your websites, you will soon be able to rely more on automatic machine translation to give accurate information about your brand, products and services to customers speaking other languages. It may one day also allow multilingual pre-sales and post-sales support through real-time translation technology. This will make communicating with local markets around the world even easier and cheaper.

Key Points

▶ The number of people able to get online will boom

▶ Mobile usage will grow phenomenally, changing the way customers behave online

▶ You need to be prepared for even more digital change, as e-marketplaces change and new digital sales channels emerge

▶ Be ready to capitalise on changes in technology that can make your business more efficient.

Resources

If you'd like more data on these disruptive trends, check out **http://www.growglobal.com/growfast.**

Chapter 9

Your International Digital Journey Starts Here

We should be using e-commerce. Encouraging 6 million, 16 million or 60 million small businesses to get benefit [to] sell globally and buy globally. This is the future and it works.

Jack Ma, Alibaba, World Economic Forum, Davos 2018[48]

What Does Your International Digital Future Look Like?

It should be looking bright and optimistic by now. You should be aware of how many customers are out there all over the globe, ready and waiting to buy your product, and also the key stages you need to go through to make it happen. There has never been an easier time to sell internationally, and with my 6-step method, there should be no stopping you. There is literally a world of opportunity out there and I've seen companies just like yours, big and small, make it happen.

I know there is a lot to think about, and it can seem overwhelming to start with, which is why I've broken down your growth journey into manageable steps. I would encourage you to break these steps down even further into bite-sized chunks.

Are You Ready to Take the Next Step?

If you're totally new to international growth, don't be paralysed into inaction and get stuck in the **Procrastinate** stage. You've already done **Step 1: Get Aware**, so move straight into **Step**

2: Get Ready and you'll see improvements to your business right away. You're only 5 more steps away from unstoppable international digital growth! Where this will take you is up to you – the sky is really the limit!

If you've already started your international digital journey, pinpoint exactly where you are right now. Then go back through the Grow Global Method, step-by-step, and fill in any gaps in your approach, so that you can boost your international leads and sales even further.

It's been so exciting to share everything I've learnt with you and to equip you with my method for fast international growth. You can start work tomorrow and expand your business all around the digital world. I've given you the key to not only improving the financial future of your business, but also enriching your life as you learn more about different countries and communicate with more customers and clients from different countries.

I hope I have inspired you to seize the opportunity and build your own international digital future.

For exclusive bonus resources to help you get started, feel free to check out my website at **www.growglobal.com/growfast.** As well as tools and templates, you can register for my upcoming webinars, so I look forward to meeting you in the digital world. I'm a regular guest speaker at business forums and seminars around the world, helping businesses just like yours to take the next step on their international digital journey. So, wherever you are, I'd love to meet you in the real world too!

And finally, I hope that one day soon, the ability to grow globally via digital channels will be accessed by businesses all over the world, and it can be used to both lift many families out of poverty and positively boost digital skills in developing countries.

Thanks for reading.

Let me know how you get on using #GrowGlobal on social media and if you need any help along the way.

Good luck!

Sarah x

WHAT NEXT?

Now that you've read the book, you'll no doubt have stacks of ideas and tons of questions.

Start Your Journey Today

What are you actually going to do today?

I want you to swing into action right now, so you don't just glide away or fall back into the **Procrastinate** stage... act now and jump straight on to **www.growglobal.com/growfast** to:

- Get your bonus material, including the latest facts and figures on the international digital world and the digital future, as well as templates mentioned in the book

- Complete your 'Am I Ready to Grow Global?' diagnostic to accurately assess exactly where you are starting from on your international digital journey

- Register for one of my free webinars or Facebook Lives to keep up-to-date and keep on learning!

- Join our exclusive Facebook Group 'Grow Fast, Grow Global' to be the first to be invited to new events I host. You will also get special Facebook Lives from me, hints and tips and updates as this is such a fast-moving area, and meet with other liked-minded businesses going through their international digital journey.

Kick-Start Your Journey To International Growth

Enrol in my Grow Global online courses

My comprehensive online courses have been specifically designed to speed up the progress of your journey to global growth. Find out exactly how to put everything you have learnt by reading *Grow Fast, Grow Global* into practice with videos, slideshows, online demos, activity worksheets, reading lists and even more resources. I have been running my five game-changing workshops for over 5 years in the UK, but have just made them available online to help businesses grow globally, wherever they are in the world. I have created five different courses, one for each of the core digital sales channels. Each course is geared for businesses who are ready to plan and implement a new digital sales channel, and will supercharge their growth by giving them the support they need to get it right first time.

The five online courses to work through are:

- International Websites for Global Growth
- International E-commerce for Global Growth
- International E-marketplaces for Global Growth
- International S-commerce for Global Growth
- Working with Online Partners for Global Growth.

Find out more and sign up at **www.growglobal.com/growfast.** If you are not sure which course you are best suited to, get in touch on **growfast@growglobal.com** and I can point you in the right direction.

Join my Grow Global Growth Accelerator Programme

My accelerator growth programmes are perfect for business with ambitions to grow fast by using digital channels. They will give you expert help to take you through the complete process and make sure that you quickly achieve your goal of increased international online sales and avoid all the pitfalls.

These programmes follow the exact 6-step method used in *Grow Fast, Grow Global,* taking you through each step in more detail and showing you how to implement them. In addition to the videos, slideshows, online demos, activity worksheets, reading lists and even more resources, you will get webinars, online group workshops and one-on-one sessions with me, so that I can answer your specific questions and review your progress. Both programmes will help you to realise your digital and international ambitions faster and more certainly than if you were doing it on your own – taking you one step closer to unstoppable international growth.

We have two groundbreaking programmes:

- Get World Class – this takes you through the first 3 steps of my method from this book **(Get Aware, Get Ready and Get Started)**

- Grow Global – which takes you through the second 3 steps of my method from this book **(Get Strategic, Get Building and Get Performing)** and introduces you to our amazing team of international implementation experts in our Grow Global Network.

To find out more and apply for either the Get World Class Programme or Grow Global Programme, go to **www.growglobal. com/growfast.** If you are not sure which of these options is best for you, please get in touch on **growfast@growglobal.com.**

Keep In Touch

If you make an international online sale or close an international lead from your website or social media, let me know by using #growglobal on Facebook, Twitter, LinkedIn or YouTube.

Grow Global: **www.growglobal.com** and **@growglobal**

Sarah Carroll: **www.sarahcarroll.com** and **@iamsarahcarroll**

If you've loved *Grow Fast, Grow Global*, I'd be so happy if you would review it on Amazon and social media and share how it has transformed your business.

Thanks for reading *Grow Fast, Grow Global*!

DEDICATION

When I look back at how *Grow Fast, Grow Global* has come into existence, I realise it was the 'book in me', and reflects the tapestry of my life, from the time when I was a toddler to the latest client meeting I have had...

So, thank you to:

- Nan – for showing me a world outside of the UK, sparking my love of languages and travel, and introducing me to our twin French family, the Lurdos, who have hosted me so many times.

- Joe – my truly wonderful son and travel companion. We've already travelled and taken on the world together and I'd go to the ends of the Earth for you. You have more application and determination than me, and I am so proud of you.

- David – my brother and sounding board, who always nudges me in the right direction, bringing life to my business and personal brands and this book cover, as well as bringing my gorgeous nieces and nephews, Matilda, Samuel, Nathaniel, Alexander and Iris into the world.

- Mum and Dad – who I miss every single day. Thanks for giving me the positive, inclusive worldview I have, and for nurturing my grit and resilience.

- Daniel and Andrew – for giving me the impetus to take my vision to the world now (and not never).

- Imogen and Debbie-Leigh – for their loyal support and assistance, never flinching when I come up with the next big project (like writing a book).

- My adorable friends and family – for giving me plenty of space and a welcoming place to write from Walthamstow to the Witterings via Cape Town, where it first started in earnest.

- Lynne and Lizzie – my writing buddies, on the same timeline, for making it seem normal to be writing a book.

- David, Estelle, Niamh, Iain, Angeline and Audrey – my test readers, who dived in wholeheartedly with astute and wildly different observations, so that every single page of the manuscript had comments on it.
- Leila and Ali – wonderful, bubbly editors, and world class without a doubt.
- Niamh, Cressida, Barney, Helen, Patrick and Robert – my A+ clients, who've been an absolute pleasure to know and work with and allowed me to share their success stories with you in this book.
- All my wonderful and positive clients, who've put their best foot forward and embraced the new international digital world and reaped its rewards.

Love you all

Sarah x

REFERENCES

1. United Nations Conference on Trade and Development. (UNCTAD), "Information Economy Report 2017," October 2017. [Online]. Available: http://unctad.org/en/pages/PublicationWebflyer.aspx?publicationid=1872. [Accessed November 2017].

2. Accenture, "Digital Disruption Growth Multiplier," 2016. [Online]. Available: https://www.accenture.com/gb-en/insight-digital-disruption-growth-multiplier. [Accessed November 2017].

3. Huffington Post, "Citizens of the Internet", January 2014. [Online]. Available: https://www.huffingtonpost.com/axelle-tessandier/citizens-of-the-internet_b_4495550.html January 2014 [Accessed November 2017].

4. OECD, "Entrepreneurship At A Glance," September 2017. [Online]. Available: http://www.oecd.org/std/business-stats/entrepreneurship-at-a-glance-22266941.htm. [Accessed January 2018].

5. Internet World Stats, "World Internet Users and 2018 Population Stats," February 2018. [Online]. Available: http://www.internetworldstats.com/stats.htm. [Accessed February 2018].

6. Worldometers, "Current World Population," November 2017. [Online]. Available: http://www.worldometers.info/world-population/. [Accessed November 2017].

7. International Monetary Fund, "World Economic Outlook Database," October 2016. [Online]. Available: https://www.imf.org/external/pubs/ft/weo/2016/02/weodata/index.aspx. [Accessed January 2017].

8. International Monetary Fund, "World Economic Outlook - Subdued Demand - Symptoms and Remedies," October 2016. [Online]. Available: http://www.imf.org/external/pubs/ft/weo/2016/02/pdf/text.pdf. [Accessed January 2017].

9. EY, "Hitting the Sweet Spot," 2013. [Online]. Available: http://www.ey.com/Publication/vwLUAssets/Hitting_the_sweet_spot/%24FILE/Hitting_the_sweet_spot.pdf. [Accessed November 2017].

10. Miniwatts Market Group, "Internet Usage Statistics The Internet Big Picture" December 2017. [Online]. Available: http://www.internetworldstats.com/stats.htm. [Accessed February 2018].

11. Miniwatts Market Group, "Internet World Users By Language," December 2017. [Online]. Available: http://www.internetworldstats.com/stats7.htm. [Accessed February 2018].

12. EMarketer, "E-commerce Will Pass a Key Milestone This Year," July 2017. [Online]. Available: https://retail.emarketer.com/article/ecommerce-will-pass-key-milestone-this-year/596e4c8cebd40005284d5ccd. [Accessed November 2017].

13. EMarketer, "Worldwide Retail and Ecommerce Sales: eMarketer's Estimates for 2016–2021," July 2017. [Online]. Available: https://www.emarketer.com/Report/Worldwide-Retail-Ecommerce-Sales-eMarketers-Estimates-20162021/2002090. [Accessed November 2017].

14. Ethnologue, "How many languages are there in the world?," 2017. [Online]. Available: https://www.ethnologue.com/guides/how-many-languages. [Accessed November 2017].

15. British Council, "The English Effect," 2013. [Online]. Available: https://www.britishcouncil.org/sites/default/files/english-effect-report-v2.pdf. [Accessed January 2017].

16. Statistics Canada, "English, French and official language minorities in Canada," August 2017. [Online]. Available: http://www12.statcan.gc.ca/census-recensement/2016/as-sa/98-200-x/2016011/98-200-x2016011-eng.pdf. [Accessed November 2017].

17. Instituto Cervantes, "El Espanol: Una Lengua Viva," 2017. [Online]. Available: https://cvc.cervantes.es/lengua/espanol_lengua_viva/pdf/espanol_lengua_viva_2017.pdf. [Accessed November 2017].

18. CNN, "Hispanics in the US Fast Facts," April 2017. [Online]. Available: http://edition.cnn.com/2013/09/20/us/hispanics-in-the-u-s-/index.html. [Accessed November 2017].

19. We Are Social, "Global Digital Report 2018," January 2018. [Online]. Available: https://wearesocial.com/blog/2018/01/global-digital-report-2018. [Accessed February 2018].

20. ITU, "ICT Facts and Figures 2017," July 2017. [Online]. Available: http://www.itu.int/en/ITU-D/Statistics/Pages/facts/default.aspx. [Accessed November 2017].

21. Google, "Mobile-first Indexing," November 2016. [Online]. Available: https://webmasters.googleblog.com/2016/11/mobile-first-indexing.html. [Accessed November 2017].

22. Pitney Bowes, "Pitney Bowes 2016 Global Online Shopping Study," 2016. [Online]. Available: https://www.pitneybowes.com/us/2016-shopping-study.html. [Accessed November 2017].

23. Statistica, "Mobile Retail Commerce Revenue Worldwide," 2017. [Online]. Available: https://www.statista.com/statistics/324636/mobile-retail-commerce-revenue-worldwide/ /. [Accessed November 2017].

24. GSMA, "Half The World's Population Is Connected By Mobile Internet," November 2016. [Online]. Available: http://www.gsma.com/newsroom/press-release/half-worlds-population-connected-mobile-internet-2020-according-gsma/ . [Accessed November 2016].

25. Investopedia, "Stock Exchanges Around The World," [Online]. Available: https://www.investopedia.com/financial-edge/1212/stock-exchanges-around-the-world.aspx. [Accessed February 2018].

26. Alexa, "Top 500 Website In The World," [Online]. Available: http://www.alexa.com. [Accessed October 2017].

27. DigiDay, "$17 Billion In One Day," November 2016. [Online]. Available: https://digiday.com/social/17-billion-one-day-alibaba-turned-chinas-singles-day-shopping-bonanza/. [Accessed October 2017].

28. Facebook OECD The World Bank, "Future of Business Survey," December 2017. [Online]. Available: https://futureofbusinesssurvey.org. [Accessed January 2018].

29. Gov.uk, "Helping Every British Business Become A Digital Business," [Online]. Available: https://www.gov.uk/government/publications/uk-digital-strategy/4-the-wider-economy-helping-every-british-business-become-a-digital-business. [Accessed November 2017].

30. Big Commerce, "E-commerce Trends," 2017. [Online]. Available: https://www.bigcommerce.com/blog/ecommerce-trends/. [Accessed November 2017].

31. W3Techs, "Usage of content management systems for websites," November 2017. [Online]. Available: https://w3techs.com/technologies/overview/content_management/all. [Accessed November 2017].

32. BuiltWith, "CMS Usage Statistics," November 2017. [Online]. Available: https://trends.builtwith.com/cms. [Accessed November 2017].

33. Shopify, "Shopify University," February 2018. [Online]. Available: https://ecommerce.shopify.com/c/payments-shipping-fulfilment/t/multiple-currency-check-out-402061. [Accessed February 2018].

34. WooCommerce, "WooCommerce," February 2018. [Online]. Available: https://woocommerce.com/. [Accessed February 2018].

35. E-commerce Foundation, "Rise of the Global Marketplaces," 2016. [Online]. Available: https://www.ecommercewiki.org/wikis/www.ecommercewiki.org/images/6/6d/Democratization_of_Marketplaces.pdf. [Accessed November 2017].

36. PwC, "Total Retail 2017," 2017. [Online]. Available: https://www.pwc.com/gx/en/industries/assets/total-retail-2017.pdf. [Accessed February 2018].

37. Marketing To China, "Ultimate Guide To Social Commerce On WeChat," May 2017. [Online]. Available: https://www.marketingtochina.com/ultimate-guide-social-commerce-wechat/. [Accessed November 2017].

38. Tek Eye, "How Many Websites Are There In The World?," September 2017. [Online]. Available: http://tekeye.uk/computing/how-many-websites-are-there. [Accessed November 2017].

39. Internet Live Stats, "Google Search Statistics," 2017. [Online]. Available: http://www.internetlivestats.com/google-search-statistics/. [Accessed November 2017].

40. Internet Live Stats, "Total number of Websites," November 2017. [Online]. Available: http://www.internetlivestats.com/total-number-of-websites/. [Accessed November 2017].

41. World Wide Web Size, "The Size of the World Wide Web (The Internet)," November 2017. [Online]. Available: http://www.worldwidewebsize.com/. [Accessed November 2017].

42. GS Statcounter, "Search Engine Market Share," January 2018. [Online]. Available: http://gs.statcounter.com/search-engine-market-share. [Accessed February 2018].

43. We Are Social, "Three Billion People Now Use Social Media," August 2017. [Online]. Available: https://wearesocial.com/blog/2017/08/three-billion-people-now-use-social-media. [Accessed October 2017].

44. Google, "Think With Google," 2017. [Online]. Available: http://www.thinkwithgoogle.com. [Accessed October 2017].

45. Entrepreneur, "How to Create a Multilingual Website," December 2012. [Online]. Available: https://www.entrepreneur.com/article/224742 [Accessed November 2017].

46. Forrester, "Enhance Your Digital Capabilities," March 2014. [Online]. Available: https://www.forrester.com/report/Enhance+Your+Digital+Capabilities+With+The+Digital+Maturity+Model/-/E-RES112901. [Accessed November 2017].

47. Harvard Business Review, "The Industries That Are Being Disrupted The Most By Digital," July 2016. [Online]. Available: https://hbr.org/2016/03/the-industries-that-are-being-disrupted-the-most-by-digital. [Accessed November 2017].

48. World Economic Forum, "Jack Ma: eCommerce Is Changing the Way We Do Business," January 2018. [Online]. Available: https://youtu.be/IJCGMr9pCWQ. [Accessed February 2018].

49. ABC News, "Jeff Bezos A Down-to-Earth CEO Reaching for the Stars," September 2013. [Online]. Available: https://abcnews.go.com/Technology/jeff-bezos-amazons-earth-ceo-reaches-stars/story?id=20363682 [Accessed November 2017].

50. Cisco, "VNI Global Fixed and Mobile Internet Traffic Forecasts," February 2017. [Online]. Available: https://www.cisco.com/c/en/us/solutions/service-provider/visual-networking-index-vni/index.html. [Accessed November 2017].

51. Population Reference Bureau (PRB), "2017 World Population Data Sheet," August 2017. [Online]. Available: http://www.prb.org/2017-world-population-data-sheet[Accessed June 2017].

52. UN, "World population projected to reach 9.8 billion in 2050, and 11.2 billion in 2100 – says UN," June 2017. [Online]. Available: http://www.un.org/sustainabledevelopment/blog/2017/06/world-population-projected-to-reach-9-8-billion-in-2050-and-11-2-billion-in-2100-says-un/. [Accessed October 2017].

53. Wikipedia, "Countries by Real GDP Growth Rate," 2015. [Online]. Available: https://en.wikipedia.org/wiki/List_of_countries_by_real_GDP_growth_rate. [Accessed January 2017].

54. The Guardian, "The places in the world with the most young people, from Albania to Antarctica," August 2016. [Online]. Available: https://www.theguardian.com/world/datablog/2016/aug/12/the-countries-with-the-youngest-populations-from-albania-to-antarctica. [Accessed August 2017].

55. Mastercard, "Digital Evolution Index 2017," July 2017. [Online]. Available: https://newsroom.mastercard.com/press-releases/singapore-uk-new-zealand-and-uae-among-worlds-stand-out-digital-economies/. [Accessed November 2017].

56. The Guardian, "India Cheapest Smartphone," February 2016. [Online]. Available: https://www.theguardian.com/technology/2016/feb/17/india-cheapest-smartphone-worlds-ringing-bells. [Accessed October 2016].

57. Consumers International, "Banking On The Future," July 2017. [Online]. Available: http://www.consumersinternational.org/media/154710/banking-on-the-future-full-report.pdf. [Accessed February 2018].

58. Search Engine Watch, "Pinterest, Google or Bing: Who has the best visual search engine?," September 2017. [Online]. Available: https://searchenginewatch.com/2017/09/28/pinterest-google-or-bing-who-has-the-best-visual-search-engine/. [Accessed October 2017].

59. Web Retailer, "Multichannel Selling Through Online Marketplaces: Present and Future," February 2017. [Online]. Available: http://www.webretailer.com/lean-commerce/multichannel-selling-online-marketplaces/. [Accessed October 2017].

60. eMarketer, "Alexa, Say What?! Voice-Enabled Speaker Usage to Grow Nearly 130% This Year," May 2017. [Online]. Available: https://www.emarketer.com/Article/Alexa-Say-What-Voice-Enabled-Speaker-Usage-Grow-Nearly-130-This-Year/1015812. [Accessed October 2017].

61. Ovum, "Virtual digital assistants to overtake world population by 2021," May 2017. [Online]. Available: https://ovum.informa.com/resources/product-content/virtual-digital-assistants-to-overtake-world-population-by-2021. [Accessed October 2017].

62. Forbes, "Optimizing For Voice Search Is More Important Than Ever," November 2017. [Online]. Available: https://www.forbes.com/sites/forbesagencycouncil/2017/11/27/ optimizing-for-voice-search-is-more-important-than-ever/. [Accessed November 2017].

63. Facebook, "Introducing DeepText: Facebook's text understanding engine," June 2016. [Online]. Available: https://code.facebook.com/posts/181565595577955/introducing-deeptext-facebook-s-text-understanding-engine/. [Accessed October 2017].